PENGUIN ANAN

VIPASSANA

Shonali Sabherwal is a macrobiotic nutritionist, chef, gut expert and author from Mumbai who has practised Vipassana for twenty-five years. She firmly believes that her life changed after her first Vipassana course in 1996. Her immense capacity to chase her dreams, ability to reach out to her clients in the lifestyle-disease space and a connection to a universal consciousness come from her meditation practice. Her previous works include the bestsellers *The Detox Diet*, *The Beauty Diet* and *The Love Diet*.

Phone: 9819035604
Email: shonaalii@macrobioticsindia.com
Website: www.soulfoodshonali.com
Instagram: Soulfoodshonali
Facebook: https://www.facebook.com/ShonaliSabherwalSoulFood
Twitter: Sh_oulfood

Vipassana

The Timeless Secret to
Meditate and Be Calm

Foreword by
THE DALAI LAMA

Shonali Sabherwal

Bestselling author of *The Detox Diet*

PENGUIN
ANANDA

An imprint of Penguin Random House

PENGUIN ANANDA

USA | Canada | UK | Ireland | Australia
New Zealand | India | South Africa | China

Penguin Ananda is part of the Penguin Random House group of companies
whose addresses can be found at global.penguinrandomhouse.com

Published by Penguin Random House India Pvt. Ltd
4th Floor, Capital Tower 1, MG Road,
Gurugram 122 002, Haryana, India

First published in Penguin Ananda by Penguin Random House India 2021

Copyright © Shonali Sabherwal 2021
Foreword copyright © The Dalai Lama 2021
Afterword copyright © Sunil Nayak 2021

All rights reserved

10 9 8 7 6 5 4 3 2 1

The views and opinions expressed in this book are the author's own and the
facts are as reported by her which have been verified to the extent possible,
and the publishers are not in any way liable for the same.

ISBN

Typeset in Sabon by Manipal Technologies Limited, Manipal
Printed at

This book is sold subject to the condition that it shall not, by way of trade
or otherwise, be lent, resold, hired out, or otherwise circulated without the
publisher's prior consent in any form of binding or cover other than that in
which it is published and without a similar condition including this condition
being imposed on the subsequent purchaser.

www.penguin.co.in

*This book is dedicated to
my mother,*

*and
to Shri S.N. Goenka,
who brought Vipassana back to India after it had been
lost for 2500 years,*

*and
to the Bodhisattva in you*

'Dharma is not Hindu nor Buddhist,
Not Sikh, Muslim, Catholic or Jain.
Dharma is purity of heart,
peace, happiness, serenity.'

—Hindi *doha* by S.N. Goenka,
The Gracious Flow of Dharma

'I'm not trying to repeat the sagas. I make my own stories and I'm very obsessed with not being nostalgic, because I think that 90 per cent of the world is too nostalgic. They don't have the courage to face the present and make stories that are relevant today, about life today . . . I want people to do more of that.'

—Björk

CONTENTS

FOREWORD

The mind is highly complex. There are a great variety of events that make up our mental world, including the many destructive emotions that give rise to our suffering. The most effective way to deal with these is to make constructive use of the mind itself. Accumulation of material wealth or drugs or alcohol will not bring about a more positive mind.

The most effective way to deal with mental pain is to reduce our negative emotions and enhance their opposites—positive emotions like loving kindness and warm-heartedness. However, we first need to calm the mind. The practice of Vipassana, as widely taught today, is an effective method for calming the mind, making it more sober and sensible.

In my own experience, nurturing concern for others brings a deep sense of joy and fulfilment. Often it is excessive self-focus that prevents us from living joyfully, with purpose and serenity. I therefore recommend combining Vipassana with a meditation practice that cultivates kindness and compassion towards others.

In this book, Shonali Sabherwal explains the form of Vipassana practice introduced by the late Shri S.N. Goenka. The book shares her personal journey into the practice of Vipassana and how she has benefited from it. I commend the author for her hard work and hope readers will find it valuable.

The Dalai Lama

INTRODUCTION

'All the world's a stage,
And all the men and women merely players;
They have their exits and their entrances;
And one man in his time plays many parts,
His acts being seven ages.'

—William Shakespeare

I believe that our lives on this earth are exactly that: we are mere participants in a play or many small acts of a play. While we go through the trials, tribulations and joyful moments of life, our only goal is to live with the human qualities of kindness and compassion and be in a state of love; living in the moment and being of service to others. I am doing this today after twenty-five years of following a technique that Siddhartha Gautam Buddha introduced to India 2500 years ago (and I say this with no attachment to ego). But I am proud of the technique that helps us to come out of negativity (suffering and misery).

Let's not forget the fact that it can also help you to come out of the cycle of birth and death (you can choose to believe it or not, but do read on) and that it exists right here. However, most of us choose to live in ignorance.

There are many disciplines that teach us how to make our lives more meaningful in order to live a better-quality, more healthy, stress-free, productive and content life. Without sounding pessimistic, death is a constant and the same for everyone. To quote Shahzeb Afzal, 'Death is a great leveller; time brings all luxuries of life to an end. All feelings of superiority in man are only an illusion and self-deception.'[1] The great question of life is not, 'How do we face life and live in this world?' It is, 'How will I face death and where will I live in the next world?'[2] There is no institution, except perhaps the technique of Vipassana, that teaches us how to have a 'quality death'. What do I mean by this? I simply mean that, at the time of our death, we should be able to look at our life and say to ourselves that we have truly lived a life, rising above our own negativities, to teach us the true meaning of dying peacefully and not fear what lies beyond death.

There is a fear attached to death because of the unknown. Many philosophical systems question what happens to us after dying. For this—with all the reading and studying that I have done on the subject—we must first experience our own 'life force' in order to know what happens to us after we exit the earth. I don't want to take a stand at this point—till you read through on what happens to us after we exit the earth—yet. But it will become clear as you read on.

I remember a hot sunny day, sitting at the Otters Club pool (Mumbai) with my school friend Preeti. She asked me, 'So Shunnu, what are your future plans? Where do you see yourself in twenty years?' And my answer was so spontaneous, 'I see myself serving or perhaps running a Vipassana centre and meditating.' She asked me, 'How come?' And to that I said, 'I am truly tied to checking out of these lives that I keep coming back to replay my dramas'. She started laughing. Preeti reminds me of the comedian and actor Jerry Lewis. She looks like him (could pass off as his daughter), so she gestured to me with her hands and eyes while saying, 'Really, Shunnu? I mean, seriously, check out. That's your plan?' I said, 'Yes, that's my future.' I didn't mean it in an escapist way. I meant it in a very tied-to-a-larger-purpose-of-my-life way. I live my life thinking this way all the time.

'It is not in our hands to outdo death, but it is in our bodies to create the best version of ourselves so that we leave behind a legacy wherein our spirit is cherished, not because of the fame that we have amassed, but because of who we have become.'[3]

PART ONE

HAPPINESS AND ME

Pursuing Happiness

Matthieu Ricard, a Buddhist monk, in his TED talk 'What Is Happiness'[1] said, 'No one wakes up in the morning and says, "May I suffer the whole day."' Consciously or not, directly or indirectly in the short or long term, whatever we do, whatever we hope, whatever we dream, is somehow related to a deep and profound desire for well-being or happiness. If you look for the definition of happiness, some people say, 'I only believed in remembering the past, imagining the future, never the present'. Some people say, 'It's the quality of the freshness of the present moment'. And that left Henri Bergson, the French philosopher, to say, 'All great thinkers of humanity have left happiness in the vague so that each of them could define their own terms.' In the Buddhist view, well-being is a deep sense of serenity and fulfilment. A state that pervades and underlies all emotional states and all the joys and sorrows that can come one's way. Can we have this kind of well-being while being sad? In a way, why not? He gives the example of waves coming near the shore. When you are at the bottom, you hit the bottom. You hit the solid rock. When you are surfing at the top, you are elated. So, when you go from elation to depression, there is no depth. Now, if you look at the high sea, there might be a beautiful, calm ocean, like a mirror. There might be storms, but the depth of the ocean is still there, unchanged. So now, how is that? It can be a state of being, not just a fleeting emotion or sensation. Even joy: that can be the spring of happiness. But there is also wicked joy. You can rejoice in someone's suffering.

My friend Geeta, who went through a lot in life, including in her marriage as well—and did many Vipassana courses with me—always said, when we did a course together, that Vipassana made it possible to weather the storms. It gave her a rudder and even though there were so many storms on the surface, her inner being was grounded and the outside environment did not affect her. As I have gone through life, I have realized that no matter what you have—riches, fame, success, power, freedom, you name it—the ultimate state of happiness is within you and within your own mind. I think the best investment I made in my life was investing in my mind, by engaging in Vipassana meditation (apart from engaging in comedy: seeing Ellen DeGeneres, Steve Martin, Bette Midler saved me many, many times from losing my mind). It's given me a treasure trove of happiness that no amount of success, power, money, a partner or anything could. Just four weeks, twenty minutes a day of caring and mindful meditation brings a structural change in the brain.[2]

The Purpose of Life, by His Holiness the Dalai Lama[3]

The purpose of life is to be happy. Right from birth, every human being wants happiness. Neither social conditioning, education nor our particular faith affects this. We simply desire contentment. I don't know whether the universe—with its countless galaxies, stars and planets—has a deeper meaning or not, but it is clear that we face the challenge of making a happy life for ourselves. So it is important to discover what will bring about the greatest degree of happiness.

We could divide every kind of happiness and suffering into two main categories: mental and physical. Of the two, it is the mind that exerts the greatest influence on most of us. Unless we are gravely ill or deprived of necessities, our physical condition plays a secondary role. If the body is content, we virtually ignore it. The mind, however, registers every event, no matter how small. Hence, we need to devote ourselves to training it to bring about mental peace.

The greatest degree of inner tranquillity comes from love and compassion. The more we care for the happiness of others, the higher is our own sense of well-being. Cultivating a close, warm-hearted feeling for others spontaneously puts the mind at ease. It helps reduce whatever fears and gives us the strength to cope with any obstacles we encounter. It is the ultimate source of equanimity.

As long as we live, we are bound to encounter difficulties. If we lose hope and become discouraged, we diminish our ability to face them. But if we remember that everyone undergoes some form of pain and dissatisfaction in their lives, as these are part of the human condition, we will increase our determination and capacity to overcome challenges. With this realistic attitude, each new obstacle can be yet another valuable opportunity to cultivate our mind.

We may not always be able to change the situation, but we can change our relationship to it. We should strive to become more compassionate, develop genuine sympathy for others' suffering, and help them. We will think less about our own serenity and inner strength will increase.

Love and compassion bring us the greatest happiness because human nature cherishes them above all else. The need for love lies at the very foundation of human existence. It results from the profound interdependence we all share with one another. However capable and skilful an individual may be, left alone, he will not survive. However vigorous and independent one may feel during the most prosperous periods of life, during ill health, one must depend on others.

Interdependence is a fundamental law of nature. Not only higher forms of life, but also many of the smallest insects are social beings. Without any religion, law or education, they survive by cooperation based on innate recognition of their interconnectedness. The subtlest level of material phenomena is also governed by interdependence upon subtle patterns of energy. When there is an imbalance, they dissolve and decay.

It is because our own existence is so dependent on the help of others that our need for love lies at the very foundation of our existence. Therefore, we need a genuine sense of responsibility and a sincere concern for others' welfare. We must consider what we really are, that we are not machines. If we were mechanical entities, then machines could alleviate all our suffering and fulfil our needs. Since we are not solely material creatures, it is a mistake to place all our hopes for happiness on external development alone. Instead, we should consider our origins and nature to discover who we are and what we require.

Leaving aside the complex question of the creation and evolution of our universe, we can at least agree that each of us is the product of our parents. From the very moment of our conception, parental love is a key factor. We are completely dependent upon the care of our mothers from the earliest stages of our growth.

The expression of love manifests at birth, since the very first thing we do is to feed on mother's milk, we naturally feel close to our mother. Then there is the critical period of the age of three or four, during which time loving physical contact is the single most crucial factor for the healthy growth of the child. If the child is not held, hugged, cuddled or loved, its brain may not mature properly. The foundation for compassion and love starts from the beginning of life. Without it, individuals and societies break down.

My Secular Beginnings

To understand where I am today, I need to rewind a bit to my younger bhakti (path of devotion) life. It also sets the tone for this book and why I was meant to encounter Vipassana in this life and move to *gyan marg* (path of knowledge). My father and mother never prayed (at least I never saw them do it up until their seventies). My father grew up in Pakistan (pre-Partition) and even though I am not Sikh, he grew up with a leaning towards the Gurudwara as his biological mother was Sikh. My father had two mothers: his biological mother and his father's first wife who could not bear him children and found a second wife for my grandfather so they could have children. My father's biological mother got the Granth Sahib (holy book of the Sikhs) home and read the chapters every day and my grandfather started doing the same. Hence the leaning towards a Gurudwara came into play in our lives.

My earliest memories of being drawn to some kind of spirituality (I mean bhakti, or path of devotion, as Indians see it), at age six, was watching my maternal grandmother praying and my aunt Santosh (mother's sister) lighting her diya. At the age of eleven, my father told me that a new room was being furnished for my sister and me in our new home and an architect had been deployed to give us what we wanted. So he asked us what we wanted. And I replied that I'd like a temple in my room. I wanted the carpenter to make me a temple. My father didn't say anything and the carpenter made me my temple. By this time, our neighbour Neelam Rai (I am sure a mother from a past life) introduced me to Shirdi Sai Baba, so my temple was first adorned with his statue after which my grandmother gave me some more statues of Hanuman and Shiva. Then I met Mrs Gupta, an ardent Shirdi Sai Baba devotee who used to have a puja every Thursday at her home, so I would go over and we became close friends. So now, she'd come over (just to refresh your memory again and believe me, this story is going somewhere, I was about thirteen then) and we would have a small havan (an Indian sacred fire ritual) from time to time. I had not told my parents about this, as we would do it quietly in front of my newly constructed temple. They just knew that Mrs Gupta liked me and would come over. Also, she was a good maths teacher, so they probably thought we were doing maths together, till one day when a havan or *homam* (Indian prayer ceremony with oblations made to the fire) was in progress. My father opened the door. We were chanting and he looked at us and closed the door. No one asked me anything at all. But I am told he went and told my mother that he feared I was going the godly way, as I was only thirteen years old. Anyway, this path of bhakti went on for a while.

I always maintain that even though I ended up being a writer, my reading habits were not inculcated by my parents, but by my uncle Shiv (mother's brother) and by watching my friend Payal Sampat read a lot. I started really hitting the books when I was fourteen; by the time I was twenty-one, I went on a sort of binge with my spiritual reading. My first spiritual book was one written by Jiddu Krishnamurti. I was fascinated by the principles of the Theosophical movement. I then read interpretations of the Bhagavad Gita. My aunt introduced me to the teachings of Rajneesh and I also became immersed in the teachings of *Advaita* and wondered why Ramana

Maharshi kept saying 'you are not the doer'. I knew I was on the path of knowledge or 'gyan marg' as we Indians call it and a lot of confusion started coming in. Questions like, Who am I? Does a higher power self-exist? Is there a soul? What is our purpose as human beings on this planet? Why am I here? started cropping up in my mind. Travelling on trains to college (St Xavier's, Mumbai) with Jiddu Krishnamurti in my hand, I devoured every theory he was putting forth. I looked around me and saw all these people and wondered how many of them felt the same way. My mind would go back to that *Amar Chitra Katha* (book of stories and Indian mythology) story of 'The Buddha' and images of how he decided to leave home to discover the true meaning of life and his story would flash back and forth.

On one hand, I saw my grandmother and aunt steeped in bhakti and on the other hand, all these books were making me question who I was. Was there a 'self' or a 'soul'? Jiddu Krishnamurti kept saying to see things 'as they are.' I felt the rope of bhakti leaving me. I no longer wanted to chant the name of Hanuman or the Chalisa 108 times on my prayer beads or bathe Lord Shiva with milk. This was not out of any aversion or anything, but I was intrigued by all these spiritual gurus telling me to look within, understand my thoughts and live in the moment. I read a lot of books about quantum physics, understanding the phenomenon of matter, the universe and our role as humans in it. I was also fascinated with many Western writers: one of my favourites was Gary Zukav. I read about the Chakra system by Anodea Judith and wanted to delve into becoming a Chakra expert. By the time I left for the US to do my master's programme, I can safely say a seed had been sown for things to come.

Back in India, after four and a half years in the US, I got married, but the marriage started showing signs of not going anywhere; to focus on that aspect of my life would not do justice to this book. But this I can say safely: when you go through a tough phase in your life, that's when things are shaken up enough to warrant change. I always maintain my marriage was like my Mahabharat (an epic in India that was about a war between two clans).

Once during my yoga class, my teacher was trying very hard to help me do away with the pain I had developed in my lower back. My family had put it down to some kind of anathema I had inherited from some old family wound, but deep down inside me, I knew I was stressed. My marriage was falling apart and at this point I was not ready to give it up. I knew it was all the stress I was carrying and holding on to emotions. After my yoga class—and I remember this day distinctly—something drew me to the notice board. Ordinarily, I would not go past the notice board. I knew there were some proverbs, wise sayings, etc., but I never made time to read them; I always wanted to dart into a rickshaw and head home. I had quit my job because of my fainting spells (low haemoglobin) at work and decided to recover from this bout of low haemoglobin, also the result of stress and nothing else.

My eyes were drawn to one poster in particular and remain fixated on it for a while. I cannot describe the moment because I felt I was deliberately drawn to read this poster. Here is what it was all about: it listed upcoming Vipassana courses at the Vipassana International Academy in Igatpuri. I knew somehow that deep down inside I had to make it, plan for it. With this thought I left for home. In the mid-1990s, there was no such thing as post-traumatic stress disorder (PTSD), or no one really brought it up or considered I may be going through it. Even though I was seeing a psychologist, she was trying her bit to get me and my husband back together. She wasn't plugged into the trauma I was going through. I was just dealing with it somehow and managing to do my best.

I had time on hand and decided to enrol in a Vipassana course. I knew it meant giving up ten days and being in silence. My yoga teacher Bubble Sahani said it would make me an introvert. But something felt right about doing the course. I did not read much about it. I just knew that my time had come to go for a course. I landed at the campus in Igatpuri, which was the first ever campus set up for a Vipassana course in India. My friend Neema, whom I met for the first time at this course, was behind the desk enrolling everyone. I introduced myself, we looked into each other's eyes and knew this was a lifetime connection. We are friends to this date. She progressed very fast on the path of Vipassana while I've taken my time. But Neema remains my modern-day Vipassana mentor and every course

I attend is not complete without a talk from her, on Dhamma, Dhamma and more Dhamma (Dharma in Sanskrit, Dhamma in Pali), which means 'the truth' or 'the law of nature'.

I will get into the details of a Vipassana course later on in the book, but one thing I'd like to close this introduction with is this: the day I finished the course and broke my silence, the penny dropped on all the information I got from the books I had read in my teens and twenties. I finally understood what all the philosophers were trying to say. Ramana Maharshi, Rajneeesh, Ramesh Balsekar, Shri Nisargadatta Maharaj, Paramahansa Yogananda, Jiddu Krishnamurti, Joseph Campbell and Gary Zukav: they all finally made sense. Hallelujah! I also knew this was my path, and also perhaps the one path to come out of the cycle of birth and death, and I was strongly tied to that thought. I knew my life on earth was one of many lives I had led in the past, the flow of Consciousness kept seeking form to play out its dramas to get rid of old karmas or sankharas, a new term I had encountered in Pali (the language of the Buddha). I took eight years to get out of my marriage, but when I finally got it, I moved fast. I decided to leave my marriage, as I had completed my karma there and left all behind with a lot of love. I attribute this to ten completed courses of Vipassana by the time I left my marriage.

Twenty-five years of Vipassana have changed me in ways that I cannot even begin to enumerate. I know that it makes me say this to you, before I start this book . . .

I respect and revere the bodhisattvas in whose steps I am walking, and I stay true to the knowledge I have gained and will share it through this book with you.

I will continue to remind myself that the knowledge and experience I have been through are my own, and I will be neutral in explaining this to you.

I will write with the utmost passion and use love and kindness as my guiding tools to steer you in the right direction in the hope that I may leave you with some curious thoughts regarding the meaning of life.

I will not play God in this book but remind myself that I am a mere fragment of this vast Universal energy and all I am trying to do is get you to understand the same about yourself.

May you, the reader, gain an immense amount of curiosity for this wonderful technique that Buddha has given us and learn to be free of negativity.

The moment I took stock of this thought and came from this centre, I stopped operating from a negative stance or even harbouring any negative thoughts. This moment happened to me many times during the course of my twenty-five-year-old practice, but actually became a line drawn on a rock, three years ago. This was when I had completed my one-month Vipassana course.

What's Been My Goal in Life?

As many of us are still seeking, this takes us to different paths. My definition of living my life comes from what Joseph Campbell says:

'The goal is to live with godlike composure on the full rush of energy, like Dionysus riding the leopard, without being torn to pieces and to follow your bliss.'[4]

In his definition, a hero is someone who has given his or her life to something bigger than oneself. It involves a painful evolution that is the prerequisite to greatness (I'd like to add, with no ego).

The twelve steps, as Campbell defined them, begin with a call to adventure, a challenge or quest that presents itself to an ordinary person (me) in the ordinary world. Initially, the person is afraid and refuses that call. But with guidance from a mentor or a text, they overcome their fears, cross the threshold and commit to the journey. The hero is then confronted with challenges, trials and failures, and pushed out of his comfort zone. Through these trials and tribulations, the hero learns new skills and goes through a death to take rebirth again. In the journey there are many revelations and many changes, the hero goes through atonement and the reward comes as the hero's journey becomes greater than himself. He now learns to live for the greater good of society and starts impacting the lives of others. So in a sense, the hero is returning changed.

In my case, my call to adventure began when a friend gave me a Joseph Campbell book, *The Hero's Journey*, while I was studying for my master's degree in the US at Marquette University. (Funnily, I remember that day distinctly, when John walked up to me and said, 'Sho, you've got to read this book.') Another turning point in my life.

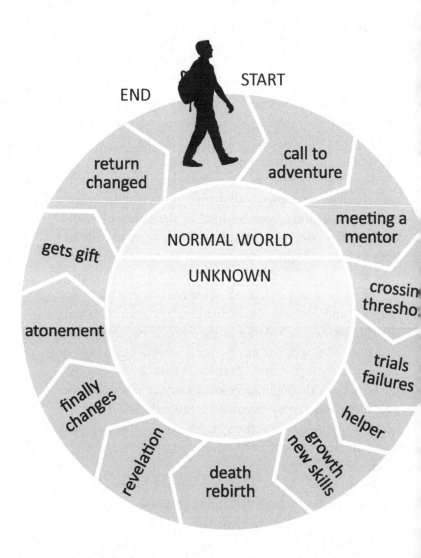

THE HERO'S JOURNEY CHART

Campbell's narrative translates into everyday existence, putting our individual struggles in a noble context. The trials and tribulations we face and survive may not seem heroic. But knowing that we grow as a result of them and that this can make us better people, makes it easier to be brave. Campbell discusses a personal journey as a spiritual quest to find what is best in ourselves, with the knowledge that the rest of humanity is on the same path of discovery. The result, or reward, is a feeling of being 'all with the world'. In this sense, the journey he is describing is a path or illumination.

Another author, Miles Neale,[5] puts Campbell's view into further perspective and divides his hero's journey into three basic stages (realizations) of 'gradual awakening'. He lays out a path that Tibetan Buddhist masters developed for lay practitioners. The goal being to go from a fearful, self-involved creature to fully human or someone who realizes all of their potential. The first realization is renunciation: he calls this 'evolutionary self-care'. In this phase, we simply become determined to abandon perceptual distortions, emotional afflictions and behavioural compulsions that cause our suffering. We decide to see clearly, rather than observing the world through the lens of hurt and insecurities which distort our vision. The determination is the first step and then we take action, learning to observe ourselves through meditation and contemplation until we become less reactive and more responsive.

The second realization is compassion or 'awakened mind'. At this point, we vow to liberate ourselves for the

VIPASSANA

benefit of others. This means helping other people see clearly and suffer less. He calls this 'radical altruism'.

The final realization is 'quantum view' or wisdom. In this state, we see below the surface of things, perceiving subtleties that aren't apparent to those blinded by their own suffering and that of others. The big picture becomes apparent and we are able to discern the connections between all things and conceive of responses and solutions to profound problems. The wisdom makes it possible for us to cause less harm: to act in ways that don't just advance our personal causes of making money and acquiring power.

While we do evolve to some degree as we age, Campbell argues that being 'conscious' of the journey is what marks the hero from the blind wanderer. The real problem is that of losing primarily thinking about yourself and your own self-protection. He says we need a transformation of consciousness.

Neale, in his book, says the hero's journey in our inherent state of blindness, separation and suffering progresses on a circular—as opposed to a linear—route made up of stages shared by myths and legends spanning all cultures and epochs. From the Buddha to Christ, Arjuna to *Alice in Wonderland*, the hero's journey is one of passing through a set of trials and phases: seeking adventure, encountering mentors, slaying demons, finding treasure and returning home to heal others.

The hero archetype is relevant to each of us—irrespective of our background, gender, temperament or challenges—because we each have a hero gene within us capable of following the path, facing trials and awakening for the benefit of others. By following your bliss, Campbell meant the bliss of the individual soul, which, like a mountain stream, reaches and merges with the ocean of universal reality. See the hero's journey diagram on page 16 to understand this view.

My Take

I would like to add here that even though just setting an intention and being determined is easy, following through without a practice like meditation becomes very difficult. It becomes mere contemplation in the kind of fast-paced lives we lead. I have tried this before I started Vipassana meditation. The transformation in consciousness becomes easier with a practice like meditation.

Why Meditate?

'You must have a room, or a certain hour or so a day, where you don't know what was in the newspapers that morning, you don't know who your friends are, you don't know what you owe anybody, you don't know what anybody owes to you. This is a place where you can simply experience and bring forth what you are and what you might be. This is the place of creative incubation. At first you may find that nothing happens there. But if you have a sacred place and use it, something eventually will happen.'

—Joseph Campbell, *The Power of Myth*[6]

I have many reasons to meditate, but the two that made me stick to the practice of Vipassana meditation are: (1) To become the finest version of myself (not said with ego) and be of service to people, which means compassion and kindness are essential and (2) to come out of the cycle of birth and death (bringing this up at the very beginning may seem weird to many, but it is the eventual goal I seek, again not attached to it in a way to have a craving for some sort of salvation). For this you also need to have mastery over the mind and not seek enlightenment in the hope that you will live on. I meditate to have spiritual freedom and yet be tied to living my life and giving to it the best version of myself.

Meditation sets the stage for what is to unfold in your life, and how you will deal with it and those that are in it.

The second point is elucidated by Martin Hägglund in his book *This Life*. In it, he says, 'In a world, both my life and the projects in which I am are *finite*. To be *finite* means two things: to be dependent on others and to live in relation to death.' He says he doesn't want an eternal life, as an eternal life is not only unattainable but is also undesirable as it would eliminate the care and passion that animate one's life. Many religious traditions talk about eternal life and eternity would make life meaningless.

Hägglund says:

> . . . what I do and what I love can matter to me only because I understand myself as mortal. The understanding of myself as mortal does not have to

be explicit and theoretical but it's implicit in all my practical commitments and priorities. The question is what I ought to do with my life—a question that is at issue in everything I do—presupposes that I understand my time to be finite. For the question of how I should lead my life to be intelligible as a question, I have to believe that I will die. If I believed that my life would last forever, I could never take my life to be at stake and I would never be seized by the need to do anything with my time. I would not even be able to understand what it means to do something sooner rather than later in my life, since I would have no sense of a finite lifetime that gives urgency, to any project or activity.

The sense of finitude—the sense of ultimate fragility of everything we care about—is at the heart of what he calls 'secular faith'. To have secular faith is to be devoted to a life that will end, to be dedicated to projects that can fail or break down. He calls it 'secular faith' because he says, 'it is devoted to a form of life that is bounded by time. To have secular faith means to be dedicated to persons and projects that are worldly and temporal. Secular faith is the form of faith that we all sustain in caring for someone or something that is vulnerable to loss. A secular faith seeks to postpone death and improve the conditions of life. The commitment to living on does not express an aspiration to live forever but to *live longer* and to *live better*, not to overcome death but to extend the duration and improve the quality of a form of life'.[7]

Why am I going on about what Hägglund is saying? Because he professes exactly that what Vipassana meditation also says, that is, to bring meditation into your life and live it through what you do. The object of secular faith—e.g. the life we are trying to lead, the institutions we are trying to build, the community we are trying to achieve—is inseparable from what we do and how we do it. Through the practice of secular faith, we bind ourselves to a normative ideal (a conception of who we ought to be as individuals and as community). He goes on to mention that the Dalai Lama summed it up perfectly when asked how a Buddhist—for whom the finite world is an illusion and who seeks to be detached from everything that passes away—can be worried about our current ecological crisis. 'A Buddhist would say it doesn't matter,' the Dalai Lama replied. This may seem surprising, since Buddhist ethics famously advocate a peaceful relation to nature and all living beings. Yet Buddhist ethics are not motivated by a concern for nature or living beings as ends in themselves. Rather, the motivation is to be released from karma, with the aim of being released from life altogether and helping others reach the same end. The goal of Buddhism is not for anyone to live on—or for the earth itself to live on—but to attain the state of nirvana, where nothing matters (from a Vipassana viewpoint, where nothing arises or passes). In the same vein, he explains with the example of the Golden Rule. To treat others as you would like to be treated is a fundamental principle in both secular and religious moral teachings. The Golden Rule, however, does not require any form of religious faith. On the contrary, a genuine care for others must be based on secular faith. If you follow the Golden Rule because you believe it is a divine command, you are motivated by obedience to God rather than by care for another person. Likewise, if you follow the Golden Rule because you believe it will yield a divine reward (e.g. the release from karma), you are acting not out of concern for the well-being of others, but rather out of concern for your own salvation. Basically, you have to care for this person as an end in itself and not because you believe it will emancipate you from some karma.

'Spiritual freedom', Hägglund explains, is the ability to ask the question: What do we do with our time? He explains we are responsible for upholding, challenging or transforming norms (social norms are not invented by us and these shape the world we live in). We are not merely causally determined by nature or these norms, but act in light of norms that one can challenge and transform. This is what it means to have a spiritual life. Where one can give our life for a principle to which one holds oneself or a cause in which one believes. Instead of being free to engage with the question of what makes our life worth living—the question of what we ought to do with our time—our lives are mortgaged to a form of labour that is required for our survival. To live a free life, it is not enough that we have a right to freedom. We must have access to the material resources as well as the forms of education that allow us to pursue our freedom and to 'own' the question of what we do with our time. What belongs to each one of us—what is irreducibly our own—is not property or goods, but the time of our lives.

In the context of the above thoughts, when we say enlightenment is possible for everyone, like it was for the Buddha or some of the more realized souls that walk this earth, one should seek enlightenment not to achieve some goal and be attached to it with a craving, but instead 'seek it to reintegrate or regroup again within communities, to give back'. I haven't seen enlightenment, I hope to someday. But I know this: Vipassana helps me live a secular faith-based life, just like Hägglund says.

2

YOU ARE ACTUALLY NOTHING

'There is only one corner of the universe you can be
certain of improving and that's your own self.'

—Aldous Huxley

What Is Vipassana?

Vipassana (In the Pali language, an ancient Indian language at one time) means 'insight' and to see things in a special way, that is, as they really are. Vipassana meditation is a technique that helps you achieve a 'fuller' life. By using the word 'fuller', I mean to be happier and to lead a meaningful life. It is mental purification through self-observation.[1]

Let's explain it in simpler terms: Vipassana helps you gain mastery over the conflict between mind and matter, like the famous expression 'mind over matter'. However, Vipassana also goes a step beyond this as it helps you understand why you create so much negativity in your life or even the craving for things around you, people, things and situations. It is the 'key' to unlock the doors of misery and sets you on the path to happiness. While this may sound like some fairy tale I am weaving at the moment, it is actually the truth. It makes you kinder, happier and a person who can take on a lot in the world we live in. Isn't that what everyone wants?

You can also go deeper with this technique, that is, use it (over time of course) to get enlightened. What does being 'enlightened' mean? The word enlightened comes from the Latin prefix 'in, into' and the word 'lux' meaning 'light'. Combine these meanings—'into the light'—and it describes a person with a sense of clarity and understanding[2]. I don't want to take this idea further here as it may trigger thoughts which, perhaps, I'd like you to understand a little later. But you can use this technique to achieve exactly what the Buddha did and yes, if you believe in the cycle of birth and death (the flow of consciousness), you can come out of that cycle. All it really means is that you have to start somewhere, and it starts with the technique of Vipassana meditation.

Vipassana is a practical, non-sectarian meditation technique, free of religious rituals, auto-suggestion, mantras or guided visualization. The technique is meant to assist in achieving the exalted objective of self-realization.

The Buddha practiced this same technique to become enlightened. In a conversation with an aged brahmin, the Buddha once explained concisely what is meant by a Buddha, an enlightened one[3]: There are not only three characteristics of a Buddha, they are also three objectives we aim at in following the Buddha's teaching. We follow the Dhamma to *fully know what should be known, to abandon what should be abandoned and to develop what should be developed.* These are the goals of the path and the three accomplishments that mark the attainment of enlightenment.

'*To fully know what should be known*'

What does this mean? It means that, when we refer to our *self*, it is as this complex structure, with body and mind. We are running from the time of birth to the time we die, attached to a sense of 'self' that is actually just an ego extension. If we ask ourselves 'what is it that I call myself?', 'I', 'me', and 'myself' are just body and mind extensions which the Buddha classifies as five aggregates: physical form, feeling, perception, volitional formations and consciousness. These are the five aggregates of 'clinging' because they are things we ordinarily cling to as, 'This is mine, this is what I am, this is my true self'.

'*To abandon what should be abandoned*'

We must abandon defilements of greed, hatred and delusion (root defilements). Greed and hatred spring ultimately from delusion and ignorance. Thus, to eliminate all the defilements, we have to eliminate ignorance.

When we know that which should be known, ignorance falls away and then greed, hatred and all other defilements fall away. We cannot accomplish this by merely having a desire to do so. We can't simply expect to think, 'I want to know that which should be known' and it immediately becomes known. That's why the whole practice of Vipassana is a process of walking on the path, like I have for twenty-five years. This does not mean you have to as well, but it does mean you need to, at least once in your lifetime, engage in it to understand how you can also become enlightened. Am I enlightened? I know that's crossing your mind at the moment. No, not yet, but I do hope to be when I check out of this life or maybe I will need more lives; having said that, I am on the path.

'To develop what should be developed'

This means to cultivate the path, *'that which should be developed, that I have developed'*—what the Buddha has developed. The path is structured in such a way that it proceeds not suddenly, not abruptly, but in a gradual step-by-step manner to help us climb the ladder to the ultimate freedom of enlightenment.

Vipassana is a universal technique—a way of knowing oneself—which is totally non-sectarian, without any unquestioning faith or connection with organized religion. The Buddha did not coin the term 'Buddhist', nor did he claim that the path he was teaching was his discovery alone. The central issue for him was two-fold: the truth of suffering, physical and mental and how to fully liberate oneself from this universal condition. The whole teaching can be summarized in a few short lines:

> *'Abstain from all unwholesome actions,*
> *Perform wholesome ones,*
> *Purify your mind.'*

—Dhammapada, 183[4]

In conclusion, Vipassana is a technique which has a very practical approach. It not only helps us pass through the vicissitudes of life in a detached way and by being completely involved, but also promotes social well-being. It is, therefore, a science not only of self-development, but also of social development. It is an art of living whereby we learn to live in peace and harmony with our own selves and with others.

To summarize the characteristic features of Vipassana:

1. It is a universal technique which can be practiced by anyone belonging to any country, caste or creed.
2. It strikes at the roots of our defilements in the unconscious mind and breaks the barrier between the conscious and unconscious layers of the mind.
3. There is no place for imagination in this technique, no verbalization of any mantra or visualization of any god or goddess or any other object. The practice starts from the experience of the apparent truth of body and mind and proceeds towards the realization of the subtle and absolute truth.
4. It is a highly individualistic and experiential method of meditation. One must walk on the path oneself. No one else can make the effort for one or liberate one from the impurities of the mind. Hence there is no 'gurudom' in this technique.
5. One reaps the benefits of this technique here and now as one progressively becomes a better individual.[5]

What Do We Seek?

As the Preamble of the Constitution of the United Nations Educational, Scientific and Cultural Organization (UNESCO) declares: 'Wars begin in the minds of men and therefore it is in the minds of men that defences of peace must be constructed'.

Dr L.M. Singhvi, former Indian high commissioner to the UK, says,

> It seems evident to me that any systematic practice which can calm and purify the mind, fill it with universal love and compassion and quicken and activate creative impulses and intelligence, is the need of our time. If elite groups in society, whether in bureaucracy or in politics or in business are able to avail themselves of the benefits of Vipassana or other forms of meditation, many problems which thwart our aspirations for the establishment of peace, harmony and happiness in the world today could be resolved. And if the ordinary citizen can derive benefits from this extraordinary technique, we may yet be able to facilitate humanity's passage to peace, progress and well-being.[6]

Everyone seeks peace. Everyone seeks harmony. Life is full of misery, of one kind or another, due to one reason or another. How can we come out of misery? How can we live harmonious lives, doing good to ourselves and doing good to others? The real cause of this misery lies deep within ourselves. Unless this deep-rooted cause of misery is eradicated, we can never experience real peace, real harmony or real happiness.

> *'Dharma is not Hindu nor Buddhist,*
> *Not Sikh, Muslim, nor Jain.*
> *Dharma is purity of heart,*
> *Peace, happiness, serenity.'*
> —Hindi doha by S.N. Goenka

Everyone who was wise and enlightened realized that the only way to eradicate misery was following the path of Dharma: *law of nature or the truth*. If one lives the life of Dharma, one is definitely coming out of misery. Dharma and misery cannot co-exist. The so-called Hindu dharma has its own rites, rituals, religious ceremonies, beliefs, dogmas, philosophies, external appearances and disciplines such as fasting. It's the same with Muslim dharma, Christian dharma, Sikh dharma and so on. But Dharma has nothing to do with all these. Sectarianism is divisive. Dharma is universal: it is supposed to unite you to everyone and everything around you.

Why Is It Relevant in Today's World?

'Each morning, the light of the sun dispels the darkness of the night. It makes no difference which part of the world it is shining upon or in which season or year. Similarly, the light of Vipassana dispels the darkness of ignorance and of misery regardless of the time or the place. Thus it is no wonder that the light of Vipassana—the light of wisdom—has proven itself of such relevance to the modern world.'

—S.N. Goenka[7]

We are going through turbulent times on many fronts. The novel coronavirus pandemic has taken over not just physically but plagues us mentally as well. If we look at 'consciousness' alone, then we realize that something's gone wrong with the 'consciousness' of human beings in general, to have manifested a virus which has forced us to stay indoors, distance ourselves socially and go through giving up a very basic principle wherein we strive to work, earn money and live life on our own terms for what is 'our freedom'. Deepak Chopra said on his Instagram handle,[8] 'To change the printout of the body, you must learn to rewrite the software of the mind'. I would like to extend this by saying, 'To change the mindsets of people, one must rewrite the software of human consciousness'.

What happened in the US to George Floyd, where police brutality towards a Black man surfaced, resulting in his death, or to Breonna Taylor, who was shot by the police without even reasoning with her or her boyfriend, or giving them a chance to explain themselves? What's happening around the world with terrorism? These are all signs of the kind of extreme negativity that can take over the human mind. In these cases, human beings have crossed thresholds no sane human would. It could be stemming from racism, depression, judgement, not having the capacity to be kind, whatever. However, on a mass level it permeates all 'consciousness' and then boom, we end up with something like a pandemic that makes us question what we have done to destroy the 'energy' around us. What we have done to poke a dark hole into the 'consciousness' of the earth, so she revolts and forces us to question everything.

Every individual has stresses and strains that their environment enforces on them. This imposes a push and pull of forces within and those outside. The world outside and especially the world today, with social media, holds us under its own trance-like magic. We may have terms to describe our cravings like ambition, goals, needs, desires, etc., but these are just terms we use to crave more and more. These are never really quenched and we just want more and more, leading us to frustration and negativity. Vipassana gives us the remedy to have healthy minds and if a bunch of us or the entire society does achieve this, then you can imagine what mass consciousness can do and even affect.

My job in the field I have chosen as my calling in this life—that of a macrobiotic nutritionist/chef—this is what I fill my time up with and it brings me to having complete *spiritual and secular freedom.* I take it very seriously and with it the role of changing the mindset of my clients who come to me with some ailment: something they soon come to realize they have created themselves on a physical and emotional front. Mental patterns impact your body's way of functioning, impairing a lot that goes on and then manifests physically. So much so that in my field, a term called 'brain inflammation' is very real. This happens when toxins start creating inflammation in the body and also affect brain tissue, leading to many issues, including anxiety, depression, mental fogginess, addiction, fatigue and many other brain-related issues. In my line of work, I know for a fact you cannot have a healthy body without a healthy brain or vice-versa. Mainstream medicine tackles symptoms and prescribes drugs, so for anxiety, depression and other mood disorders, you are provided with a prescriptive drug. A homoeopathic doctor will treat you psychosomatically, but—like foods have the capacity to heal your body and mind—rewiring the monkey mind treats the root cause of all these issues. And while I do believe diet is extremely important, meditation is the only other tool that can be used to reset the brain.

A technique like Vipassana is not just needed for one person, but for the human race as a whole, to transcend through the limitations we self-impose or have acquired by our past conditioning, whose negative patterns are carried by us throughout our lifetimes. Patterns we keep recreating over and over, without breaking them. We need a coping mechanism that will be our tool against anything that could befall us on a mental-pattern level.

Sometime back, I remember being plugged into the news because of how our state government had made a mess of one case that was all over the news. I could not get Arnab Goswami out of my living room. Every evening, I hung on to every word, every debate; so much so that in between my workday, I'd go to the television to see what's going on. It fuelled some anxiety in me and in a friend who lived in New York. Our entire discussion centred around this case. I realized that instead of calming our anxiety, news channels were feeding it instead. We were already in a pandemic that had just started, people were dying all around us and now this. It took me a lot to walk away from this madness. I stopped the daily papers, except on weekends. I realized the news had nothing much to add to my life. I'm still not getting them a year down the line. All you hear are headlines that are screaming more gloom and making you feel worse in this already dark space the world is in.

On the one hand, there is a world that has moved so far ahead: I have much more than my father had at his age. So obviously we have moved in the right direction. Yet it's also become a little worse for all of us. Fashion trends, fad diets, social media addiction, the stress of looking younger and thinner, making more money, the idea that this is not where we are meant to be, but that there is always another place we can be transported to, seem to be the order of the day. In the last one year, I have recommended four young adults, my friends' kids, to my psychologist, for different conditions, all related to fear psychosis. I feel the fact that the world is talking so much about 'mindfulness' at this time is also a sign that it is the need of the hour as a reaction to what we are all going through. Our minds just need a break.

> Remember:
> *Feeling you have no time doesn't mean you have no time.*
> *Feeling you are ugly doesn't mean you are ugly.*
> *Feeling anxious doesn't mean you need to be anxious.*
> *Feeling you haven't achieved enough doesn't mean you haven't achieved enough.*
> *Feeling you lack things doesn't make you less complete.*[9]

The Brain and Its Complexities

The blueprint for a brain disorder that may happen in your lifetime is sometimes set in the womb, and some brain disorders do happen late in life. I can say this with the utmost surety that in most cases there is also an underlying gut disorder. However, more on that later. For now, we know that in a normal scenario the brain works very well as a super-functioning machine. Lifestyle choices make a huge difference. Howard Friedman, a researcher at the University of California in Riverside and co-author of the book *The Longevity Project: Surprising Discoveries for Health and Long Life from the Landmark Eight-Decade Study*, helmed a longitudinal and a longevity study that identified factors such as strong family ties, healthy lifestyles, meaningful work and religious observance as being important to a long life. They have also found a conscientious personality to be the key.[10] While brain lesions, i.e., damaged brain tissue, neurodegenerative disorders (the progressive loss of brain cells) leading to Parkinson's, Alzheimer's, dementia, mood disorders, addictions and depression, to name a few of the myriad brain-related diseases do have real causes, in most cases, if a meditation technique is used early enough, these disorders are prevented and if not prevented then better managed.

'A meditating brain is an anti-ageing brain.'

3

CONSCIOUSNESS AND
THE BRAIN

What Is Consciousness?

Simply defined, it is the ability to experience, to feel, and yes, to think. The combination of familiarity and mystery had made consciousness a philosophical and psychological talking point for hundreds of years. Many of the most learned minds in history have tried to answer such questions as: What is the self? What is free will? And what is the function of awareness? And as our abilities to think, abstract, dream, problem-solve, imagine, consider, analyse, compute and reflect are housed in our brains, many have hoped that neuroscience would help us better comprehend the nature of consciousness.

What neuroscience had added to the discussion, however, seemed to be more about how much we aren't aware of, not only about consciousness in general, but also concerning how much information the brain manages to take in unconsciously yet still uses to help inform perception, reasoning and decision-making. The unconscious mind is

It's believed the average person has as many as **70,000** unique thoughts in a single day. This does not include thoughts that exist because of your past or stuff you have been attached to which keeps coming up.

quite adept as well at taking in sensory data and forming memories. Indeed, what we're unconscious of may have just as much power as the cognitive processes of which we are conscious.[1]

Christof Koch, PhD and CEO of the Allen Institute for Brain Science says, 'Put most simply, consciousness is a matter of being awake and aware of your surroundings'. This is a simplistic and more physical definition of consciousness. The Buddha, of course, added a whole new dimension to this meaning. Let's stay with this physical definition for a while: What in the human brain gives rise to such awareness? Koch, the neuroscientist, looked at the physicality of this definition.

When he was asked what the easiest way was to explain consciousness, this was what he said: 'It's not that hard really—it's experience. It's just having experiences. Feeling, seeing, touching, smelling, having pain, having pleasure, doing things, moving, solving something: These are all conscious experiences. It's what everyone does all the time when they are awake. It's what goes away and what you aren't doing when you are asleep.'

When asked what the challenges were of trying to study consciousness from the brain perspective, he said: 'The biggest may be trying to understand what physical things underlie consciousness. How is it possible that the brain, which is comprised of matter, can give rise to experiences? It's not clear right now. And there is no scholar that agrees on a theory of how organized matter like the human brain gives rise to experiences. It's called "mind-body problem".' Even hundreds of years ago, philosophers were trying to figure out the relationship between mind and matter in this way.

Koch further says that although we know consciousness comes from the brain—that consciousness is a product of the brain—we don't know if the brain is the only thing that gives rise to consciousness. There may be more.[2]

On a Brain Level, How Perceptions Build Into Consciousness

Andrew Newberg, MD, who in his book puts forth his studies from a neuroscience standpoint, explains how perceptions are formed. The basic functional unit of the human system is the neuron, a tiny spindly cell that—when arranged into intricately woven chains of long neural pathways—carries sensory impulses to the brain. At the basic level, sensory data enters the neural system in the form of billions of tiny bursts of electrochemical energy gathered by countless sensors in the skin, eyes, ears, mouth and nose (what the Buddha referred to as the sense doors: this is an analogy I am extending here). These neural impulses race along neural pathways, cascading like a line of falling dominoes, leaping synaptic gaps and triggering the release of chemical neurotransmitters as they carry their sensory messages toward the brain.

Once inside the brain proper, sensory information is channelled along the appropriate neural pathways. Optical input travels the pathways of the brain's visual system, for example, while impulses from the sense of smell are channelled along the olfactory circuits. Here, they are sorted, cross-referenced, amplified or inhibited, integrated with input from emotional centres and other senses and finally assembled into a perception that has a useful, individual meaning to the owner of that particular brain.

The first level of sensory processing occurs in the *primary receptive areas* dedicated to each of the sensory systems. These areas receive unprocessed input directly from the senses and assemble that raw data into rough, preliminary perceptions. These perceptions then travel to the *secondary receptive areas,* each of which is also dedicated to a specific sensory system where they are further refined.

Sensory perceptions then move to *association areas,* where the most sophisticated processing occurs. These structures are called association areas because they gather together or 'associate' neural information from various parts of the brain. At this highest level, information from a single sense is integrated with information from all the other senses to create rich, multidimensional perceptions that form the building blocks of *consciousness.* The association areas eventually tap into memory and emotional centres to allow us to organize and respond to the exterior world in the most complete way possible.

This tapping into memory and emotional centres is what Vipassana trains you to observe and not react to.

The voluntary act of a response that is generated in response to a stimulus that comes in through the six sense doors—your eyes, nose, ears, tongue, body and mind—can be negative or positive, creating a reaction stemming from two polarities: craving or aversion.[3]

How the Brain Makes up Its Own Mind

There seems to be—within the human head—an inner personal awareness, a free-standing, observant self. We have come to think of this self—with all its emotions, sensations and cognitions—as the phenomenon of the mind.

Neurology cannot completely explain how such a thing can happen: how a non-material mind can rise from mere biological functions; how the flesh and blood machinery of the brain can suddenly become 'aware.' Science and philosophy, in fact, have struggled with this question for centuries, but no definitive answers have been found and none is clearly on the horizon. Newberg attempts to ascribe definitions: the brain is a collection of physical structures that gather and process sensory, cognitive and emotional data; the mind is the phenomenon of thoughts, memories and emotions that arise from the perceptual processes of the brain. In simpler terms, brain makes the mind.

All the things the mind perceives—all thoughts, feelings, hunches, memories, insight, desires and revelations—have been assembled piece by piece by the processing powers of the brain from the swirl of neural blips, sensory perceptions and scattered cognitions dwelling in its structures and neural pathways.

Newberg says God cannot exist as a concept or as a reality anywhere else but in your mind. In this sense, both spiritual experiences and experiences of a more ordinary material nature are made real to the mind in the very same way: through the processing powers of the brain and the cognitive functions of the mind. Whatever the ultimate nature of spiritual experience might be—whether it is in fact a perception of an actual spiritual reality or merely an interpretation of sheer neurological function—all that is meaningful of human spirituality happens in the mind. In other words, the mind is mystical by default.[4]

A QUANTUM VIEW

'There is no place in this new kind of physics both for the field and matter, for the field is the only reality.'

—Albert Einstein

It is on this very point that Eastern mysticism and Western science meet. '*Tat tvam asi*' (thou art that), is the bottom line of Joseph Campbell's philosophy. There is no matter, everything is field. Separations and limitations are in our own minds.[1]

Quantum Physics and Consciousness

Going a bit deeper and taking into account what quantum physics puts forth, long before the early Greek philosophers—and certainly long before quantum physics—the sages of India knew that there was something important going on beyond the realm of the senses. Both Hindu and Buddhist seers taught—and still teach—that the world of appearances, the world we see with our senses, is maya or illusion and that something underlies this material realm, something that is more powerful and more fundamental, more 'real', even though it's completely intangible. As so many spiritual texts suggest, there is a 'higher reality' that is more fundamental than the material universe and it has something to do with consciousness.

This is also precisely what quantum physics is revealing. It suggests that at the core of the physical world there is a completely non-physical realm, whether we call it information, probability waves or consciousness. And just as we commonly say that atoms are what things are 'really' made of, if this view is correct, we would have to say that this underlying field of intelligence is, deep down, what the universe 'really' is.

NASA astronaut Dr Edgar Mitchell came to this conclusion on his return trip from space:

> In one moment, I realized that this universe is intelligent. It is processing in a direction and we have something to do with that direction. And that creative spirit, the creative intent that has been the history of this planet, comes from within us, and it is out there. It's all the same . . .
>
> Consciousness itself is what is fundamental and energy matter is the product of consciousness . . . if we change our heads about who we are and can see ourselves as creative, eternal beings creating physical experience, joined at that level of existence we call consciousness, then we start to see and create this world that we live in quite differently.[2]

What is consciousness? At some level we have that 'awareness', something within us that keeps us vigilant. Every thought, experience, action and perception forms a part of this so-called field of consciousness; this consciousness is something of the present, that is, the moment we are in and the past that is sometimes triggered by thoughts, memories and past conditioning.

Consciousness is fundamental to all we do: art, science, relationships, life; it's the constant of our lives. And yet, science has done very little to examine it deeply. However, Nick Herbert, PhD in experimental physics from Stanford University, says, 'Consciousness still remains an intellectual black hole.'[3]

Many scientists—in physics and psychology, who are still wedded to the materialist/Newtonian paradigm—dismiss consciousness as a product of brain functioning. Essentially, they say the 'me' sense of you is an 'oops' accident of evolution. And that when the brain dies, the 'oops' goes away and the packaging joins the other consumed wrappers in the dump.

Even if we turn our attention inward, we've been more interested in the content of consciousness—the stuff that populates the neuronets, including thoughts, dreams, plans, speculations—than in consciousness itself. We're interested in the images of the movie, but we forget that without the screen on which the images play, nothing would be there.

But probably the most important reason is that *consciousness doesn't fit in the Newtonian paradigm*. It's not made of the measurable stuff. You can't put a meter on consciousness. And most scientists remain immersed in the worldview split apart hundreds of years ago by Descartes: The intangible, non-physical or spiritual are forever separate from the physical. Therefore, to explain consciousness, they have only a brain-based phenomenon of chemistry and neural circuits. And in that paradigm, scientists have gone so far as to call consciousness an anomaly.

Consciousness remains a mystery; rapid advances may help pinpoint us in that direction. Philosophers have tried to answer these questions and debates are really fierce. We know consciousness arises in the brain. Christof Koch, of the Allen Institute for Brain Science, says consciousness rests in the cerebral cortex and that it's part of this sheath that gives rise to consciousness (plus intelligence and reasoning). He is striving to come up with a scientific theory of consciousness. Even if a part of the cerebral cortex is lost on a physical level, consciousness is not affected, it remains. Francis Crick (before his death in 2004)—a British neuroscientist and co-discoverer of the structure of DNA—and Christof Koch were working together on the 'binding problem', which, put simply, asks how the brain integrates different bits of information it gets: both sensory and internal. Because our experience of consciousness is derived from the data we get from lots of different systems— the visual and motor being only two—they studied claustrum (a thin bilateral structure that connects to the cortical and subcortical regions of the brain). No first-person subjective experience has been recorded of consciousness. Science is still trying to understand 'consciousness'. It's a question about how we feel on the inside. Some philosophers argue that consciousness can be explained a lot more simply. Daniel Dennett, philosopher and professor of cognitive science at Tufts University, says our brains have been designed by evolution and then redesigned by cultural evolution to give us a user-friendly system of things in the world that we deal with. The user-friendly world simplifies and distorts: if you want to know what's going on in the brain, we need to go backstage. Until recently, we did not have tools to do it. Now we are developing tools to study the brain. For the time being, the puzzle of consciousness poses more questions.[4]

The question then is: Is consciousness supreme? The Indian tradition maintains that consciousness is the basic component and everything stems from here. John Hagelin, PhD, is a renowned quantum physicist, educator, author and science and public policy expert. He says:

'The very earliest experience, the beginning of the universe you could say, is when pure consciousness, the unified field seeing itself, creates within its essentially unified nature the threefold structure of observer, observed and the process of observation. From that, at the deepest level of reality, consciousness creates creation so, yes, there is a very intimate relationship between the observer and the observed. They are ultimately united as one inseparable wholeness at the basis of creation, which is also our own innermost consciousness, the self.'[5]

Just as the physical scientists use physical measuring devices, the explorers in consciousness use *consciousness itself*, to measure consciousness. The Buddha and Indian sages—or those who are the explorers (Eckhart Tolle, Tom Campbell, Jiddu Krishnamurti, Swami Rama, Paramahansa Yogananda and many more individuals) of delving deeper into human consciousness and achieving clarity and wisdom on the realm of consciousness—apply it to our day-to-day lives. The common underlying thread in all their experiences as espoused by them is when the boundaries of the self give way to reveal that the self is everything, everywhere, all the time, suggesting that not only is consciousness not created by the brain, but also that the brain limits consciousness.

Mind over Matter

We often think that the mind has control over matter. Sure it does, but when it comes to how we react to outside stimuli, is it the mind that comes first or matter (by this I mean our bodies)?

Dr Joe Dispenza, who does a lot of research and lectures in the field of mind–body medicine and gives lectures all over the world about demystifying the mystical, has a lot to say on the subject. I have been a big fan of his work for very long now. His understanding of how mind and matter work and the fit with quantum physics is seamlessly explained in many of his books. When I look at someone who connects the dots—just like the Buddha did so many eons ago—Dr Joe Dispenza outlines it very well for a thorough understanding and it comes back to what the Buddha explained: there is no mind and matter, but pure energy.

Connecting the dots between the outer, physical world of the observable and the inner, mental world of thought has always presented quite a challenge to scientists and philosophers. To many of us, even today, the mind appears to have little or no measurable effect on the world of matter. Although we'd probably agree that the world of matter creates consequences affecting our minds, how can our minds possibly produce any physical changes affecting solid things in our lives? Mind and matter appear to be separate . . . that is, unless there's a shift in our understanding about the way physical, solid things actually exist. Dr Joe Dispenza outlines the flow of history in the quantum view of mind, matter and consciousness. Humanity first believed that the nature of the universe was orderly and thus predictable and explainable. The seventeenth-century mathematician and philosopher Rene Descartes—who developed many concepts that still have great relevance in mathematics and other fields—believed that the universe is controlled by predictable laws.

When it came to human thought, Descartes faced a challenge: the human mind possesses too many variables to neatly fit into any laws. He concluded that the study of matter was the jurisdiction of science (always matter, never mind), whereas the mind was God's instrument, so the study fell into religion (always mind, never matter). He put forth a belief system that imposed a duality between the concepts of mind and matter. For centuries, this stood as the accepted understanding of the nature of reality.

Sir Isaac Newton perpetuated this belief system. According to his 'classical' Newtonian physics model, all things were considered solid. For example, energy could be explained as a force to move objects or to change the physical state of matter. By extension, the work of Descartes and Newton established a mindset that if reality operated on mechanistic principles, then humanity had little influence on outcomes. All reality was predetermined.

Einstein did undermine this thinking. His theories set off an exploration of the puzzling behaviour of light. Scientists observed that light sometimes behaves like a wave and at other times, behaves like a particle. According to Descartes and Newton, it couldn't: a phenomenon had to be one or the other. Quickly, it became clear that the dualistic Cartesian/Newtonian model was flawed at the most basic level of all: the *subatomic* (refers to the parts—electrons, protons, neutrons and so on—that make up atoms, which are the building blocks of all things physical). The most fundamental components of our so-called physical world are both waves (energy) and particles (physical matter), depending on the mind of the observer. To understand how the world works, we had to look to its tiniest components. Out of all this, a new science was born, called *quantum physics*.

THE QUANTUM ATOM

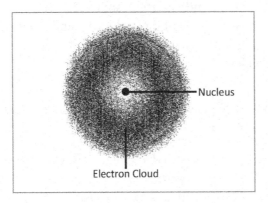

The 'new-school' quantum version of an atom with an electron cloud. The atom is 99.99999 per cent energy and .00001 per cent matter. It's just about nothing materially.[6]

THE REAL QUANTUM ATOM

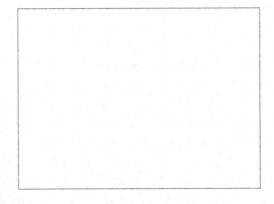

This is the most realistic model of any atom. It is 'nothing' materially, but all things potentially.

This is also what the Buddha found, but by going deeper beyond mind and matter, splitting each subatomic particle he was made of and achieving enlightenment and yet coming back to this world. And this is possible for you as well.

How Does Vipassana Allow You to Transmute Consciousness?

'Between stimulus and response is a space. In that space is our power to choose our response. In our response lies our growth and our freedom.'

—Viktor Frankl

Vipassana meditation teaches you how to tap into the *space* between a stimulus and response. In a sense the Buddha *uses consciousness to discover reality and consciousness itself* by using Vipassana as a tool. The boundaries of the self drop away and through Vipassana, you can experience reality beyond mind and matter. This is a strong statement I am making: limiting consciousness only to the brain is not an all-pervasive view of what consciousness really is. This space that crosses mind and matter is a space where I have seen 'shifts' take place in my life. What I mean by 'shift' here is that one goes through one's day-to-day life, unconditioned and not coloured by something the way you want it to be, but 'as is'. Also using these moments to change one's reality and, like Viktor Frankl says, achieving growth and freedom.

The Connection between Vipassana and Mathematics

(You can skip to Chapter 5 if you are not interested in getting on to the technicalities of connecting Vipassana to mathematics.)

Alka Marwaha, PhD, has written on the subject of Vipassana and mathematics using mathematics as a framework to prove how Vipassana works.[7] She espouses in her book that mathematics is believed to have developed in leaps and bounds after the efforts of stalwart mathematicians like Pythagoras, Euclid, Aristotle and others who existed in ancient Greece around the sixth century BC. Interestingly, Siddharth Gautama, the teacher of Vipassana, was also born in the sixth century BC in the northern region of the Indian subcontinent.

Pythagoras also visited India in his travels to search for truth and wisdom. This was the time Gautama Buddha had dispelled the darkness of ignorance through his teachings. He was also greatly influenced by the Buddha's teachings. He arrived in India as a student, but left as a teacher. On returning, he established a school where students were initiated into the teachings of philosophy, ethics, logic and mathematics. The Pythagoreans believed in the wheel of life (life and death), which is an indication of the influence of the Buddha's teachings on Pythagoras, for the Buddha also talked of *bhavachakra* or *samsara*. The confluence of mathematics and spirituality is starkly visible in the case of the Buddha and Pythagoras.

Without getting too technical, she goes on to explain every concept of Vipassana, breaking it down into formulas that prove the technique. She puts forth her views on spirituality and self-realization. She says the apparent self is made up of two entities: the body and the mind; one is tangible and the other is abstract. Thoughts are generated in the mind and converted into actions and actions are performed through the medium of the body. Actions generated by thoughts are like arrows starting from a given point and shooting like rays, but they do not disappear into oblivion. In fact, they return with powerful impact.

The modus operandi of mathematics is quite similar to the advancement on the path of Vipassana. A student of Vipassana finds that his understanding—ensuing from his initial experiences—forms the building blocks for further progress on this path. Once the base is formed, consistent and sincere effort on the path of both mathematics and Vipassana yield the desired results. The mind is the source of infinite power and energy. It contains the seed of creation as well as destruction. The stored-up energy of the mind is like an all-consuming fire, unless it is tamed and controlled to become a dispenser of light and warmth. The mind always looks to nature for inspiration. There is a great similarity in their behaviour patterns. Nature, sometimes grossly and sometimes subtly, shows that life must be followed by death and that there is a new beginning in every ending. The apparent truth is that whatever comes into being exists for a certain period of time and then perishes. In reality, every stimulus that one experiences comes to nought and at that very instant, a new stimulus takes birth only to meet its end. The process of arising and passing away takes place ceaselessly.

This is the gross reality of nature. It's important for us human beings to understand our own existence in relation to the existence of the world around us.

When we question what is our ultimate goal, how come there is someone in our heads who feels, hears, understands? Who is this self? What is the 'soul'? Is there a 'soul'? Is there birth and death? Or is it just a belief system we Indians have coined for ourselves? What we can commonly come to an agreement on, is that there is something called 'consciousness'. This is what I have sought to define in the above discussions on consciousness. However, what happens when we are no more? I asked a lot of these questions when I was younger. I never fully comprehended what the real meaning behind it all was. I used to draw this image of myself climbing uphill towards a house. The picture itself was of someone alone. We come alone and we die alone. As pessimistic as this sounds, this is our reality. Yet we collect a lifetime of impressions, arguments and a fair amount of negativity, more than feeling or generating positivity. The reality is we will go the same way we came, alone. So what's the fight all about?

The Concept of Infinity in Mathematics Related to the Ultimate State of Infinity

Marwaha explained that in order to define a number which transcends all finiteness, the symbol ∞ was coined. Just as the state of supreme bliss is greater than any happiness attained from materialistic gains, infinity is the state that is larger than the largest of the numbers one can think of. Similarly, *nibbana* (nirvana in Sanskrit)—

meaning freedom from suffering, the ultimate reality—is a state of mind which has been visualized by man to be one that is perfect in all respects and can be attained only by transcending all materialistic, mundane activities. Infinity can be compared to this state of perfection and the properties of infinity have been likewise defined. Those who attain liberation become one with it. In the exalted state of liberation, one dwells in infinite compassion, bliss, equanimity and peace and therefore, it must be true that:

$$\infty + \infty = \infty$$

The path of spirituality (what I term as secular freedom in this book)—if infinity symbolizes the ultimate truth—can be attained only by going through the range of all the finite experiences of life. Every emotion that we feel is representative of finiteness, which can be easily comprehended through close and dispassionate observation. From moment to moment, we experience different emotions. Awareness of these will lead to complete understanding of them and by overcoming them one finite step at a time, we can definitely reach the ultimate (infinite) truth.

Many beliefs and philosophies had existed before the Buddha about why human beings suffer so much mental agony, despite our best intentions and efforts to make our lives more comfortable, happy and peaceful. All unanimously agree that the attachment to the transitory world is the root cause of suffering and in order to remove suffering, one must develop detachment towards the allurements of the world. Like a scientist, the Buddha investigated the behaviour of his own mind at the deepest levels and discovered that, between the external objects and mental cravings, there is a missing link: *vedana* or sensation. The mind follows the chain of Dependent Origination:

Salayatana–paccaya phassa
Phassa–paccaya vedana
Vedana–paccaya tanha

(Dependent on the six sense doors, contact arises
Dependent on contact, sensation arises
Dependent on sensation, craving arises.)[8]

VIPASSANA AND HOW I PROVE IT WORKS

Distinction between Subconscious and Unconscious Mind

Before I dive into this section, let me make the distinction between the subconscious and the unconscious mind. In the field of psychology, the subconscious mind refers to that part of the consciousness that we are unaware of and the term was coined by Pierre Janet. It is information that we are not actively aware of in the moment, but that can influence us nonetheless, such as things that are heard, seen or remembered. The information stored in the subconscious or the preconscious mind may not be on the surface, but it is accessible. You can become aware of this information if you direct attention towards it, like in a memory recall.

The unconscious mind, on the other hand, is a term coined by Friedrich Schelling, an eighteenth-century German philosopher.[1] It refers to a part of the mind that cannot be known by the conscious mind and includes socially unacceptable ideas, wishes and desires, traumatic memories and painful emotions that have been repressed. The unconscious mind stores the primal, instinctual thoughts which we cannot deliberately access. The unconscious mind holds on to the countless memories, experiences and impressions we have collected through our lives that drive our behaviour and patterns.

I have always been a student of the fascinating aspects of the mind. I read avidly on dreams and their meanings and then—when my homoeopath asked me to relate my dreams back to her so she could understand what I was really going through in my unconscious mind—my theory of dreams being an active 'play out' of what we hold on to in our lives (or many lives) became apparent.

The so-called 'unconscious' mind is not unconscious. It is always conscious of body sensations and keeps reacting to them. While Western psychologists refer to the 'conscious' mind, the Buddha called the conscious mind a very small part of the mind. There is a big barrier between the 'conscious' mind and the rest of the mind at deeper levels. The conscious mind does not know what is happening in the unconscious mind. Because the Vipassana technique breaks this barrier when you engage in it—taking you from the surface level of the mind to the deepest levels of the mind—I could go through this process experiencing what I did and thus proving that something was indeed going on beyond a physical level which is also connected to my consciousness when I go through my courses.

The Unfolding of My Consciousness When Engaging in Vipassana, Macrobiotics and Ayurveda

Robert A. Johnson, in his book *Inner Work*,[2] says that the unconscious is a marvellous universe of unseen energies, forces and forms of intelligence—even distinct personalities—that live within us. It is a much larger realm than most of us realize, one that has a complete life of its own running parallel to the ordinary life we live day to day. The unconscious is the secret source of our thought, feeling and behaviour. It influences us in ways that are all the more powerful because they are unsuspected.

The unconscious manifests itself through a language of symbols. It is not only in our involuntary or compulsive behaviour that we can see the unconscious. It has two natural pathways for bridging the gap and speaking to the conscious mind: one is by dreams while the other is through imagination.

Many communicative efforts by the unconscious are lost on us. The unconscious bubbles to the surface in dreams, but few people have the information necessary to take their dreams seriously and understand their language. To get a true sense of who we are and become more complete and integrated human beings, we must go to the unconscious and set up communication with it. Much of ourselves and many determinants of our character are contained in the unconscious. Carl Jung, the Swiss psychologist and psychiatrist who founded analytical psychology,[3] has shown that by approaching the unconscious and learning its symbolic language, we live richer and fuller lives. We begin to live in partnership with the unconscious rather than at its mercy or in constant warfare with it.

Jung's studies and work led him to conclude that the unconscious is the real source of all human consciousness. It is the source of our human capacity for orderly thought, reasoning, awareness and feeling. The unconscious is the Original Mind of humankind, the primal matrix out of which our species has evolved a conscious mind and then developed it over the millennia to the extent and the refinement that it has today. Every capacity, every feature of our functioning consciousness, was first contained in the unconscious and then found its way from there up to the conscious level.

The unconscious is an enormous field of energy, much larger than the conscious mind. Jung compared the ego—the conscious mind—to a cork bobbing in the enormous ocean of the unconscious. He also compared the conscious mind to the tip of an iceberg that rises above the surface of the water. Ninety-five per cent of an iceberg is hidden beneath the dark, icy waters. The unconscious, like most of the iceberg, is out of sight. But it is enormously powerful and as dangerous as a submerged iceberg, if not respected.

I Am My Own Experiment in the Vipassana Technique

Every single course that I have attended, apart from engaging in the technique itself, I have vivid dream states. I would like to add here for those who have done Vipassana and are reading this book that this situation is unique to my experience and may not be happening to you. So you may not identify with it. I remember the characters, the colours and also the plot or story that unfolds in them. This happens in 1–2-hour intervals, all through the night. These dreams could be described as short movies in which I see my unconscious mind unravel. Initially, at the start of the course, the dreams make sense. They are about situations I was facing before I left for my course or people whom I know and interact with in my life: friends, family, work people, staff. But as I keep going deeper into the course and the meditation continues, the dream states start throwing up images, plots and stories not related to the day-to-day life I left behind. I know they have some meaning, that these dreams are connected to me. I've become good at remembering them. While you do a Vipassana course, you are not allowed to have a paper, pen or any writing material. So, I have started remembering my dreams with cue words I give to them when I wake up. I dream—sleep—dream—sleep. Why do I want to remember them? I do this because my homoeopathic doctor, Dr Divya Chhabra, requests me to remember them as she says they reveal deep facets to my personality and what I am going through. So, every time I am back from a course, she has sessions just to record what I remember.

You must be wondering why I am telling you all this. I am trying to further prove to you that the meditation, as S.N. Goenka says, is like operating surgically on the unconscious mind and at one point he also describes it as all the 'pus' impurities—that we may have held on to— starting to come up. I feel these dreams are my catharsis of situations I have held onto, things which I have locked into my psyche unconsciously. And because of this surgical operation on the mind, they are now given a chance to come up. In meditation (as I will explain later), we do not engage with and get lost in our thoughts, we simply observe sensations with equanimity. This allows everything to come up. While sensations are one way as you will understand, dreams become another way to purge the unconscious mind.

I dream for an hour, then wake up fresh. It is not difficult going back to sleep, but the moment I do, I start dreaming again. Whether it's a ten-day, twenty-day or thirty-day course, this dream purge starts with me on day two and continues till the second last day of the course. I have become used to this process now. And yes, it has helped me work through a lot of things in my life. I've checked with many meditators and this process does not happen to them. I don't want to say I am unique in some way. All I know is this dreaming stops on the last day when we go through something called *metta*. This also will be explained later.

The only two other times I have experienced the same kind of dream patterns is when I stayed at the Kushi Institute for all my levels of macrobiotic study. Food touches your consciousness and has a way of affecting it as well. A macrobiotic and Ayurvedic approach both talk about this; we have heard about sattvic foods and their effects on the mind. It is the same principle—and when I was pursuing my macrobiotic studies—every time I ate the food at the Kushi Institute, there began the same dream states (like at a Vipassana course) through the night. At the time I was a bit startled, but when I understood the power of 'clean eating' and studied the subject of macrobiotic foods a little more, it was evident that the foods were having an effect on my consciousness as well. This was the second time that it was proved to me that just as Vipassana took me deep into my unconscious mind, so were the 'foods' that I was eating on the macrobiotic path at the Kushi Institute impacting my flow of consciousness.

Years later—when I was at my panchakarma cleanse at Arya Vaidya Chikitsalayam (Coimbatore) I go to (I had simultaneously been doing my panchakarma every year) —I engaged in a cleansing technique called *snehapanam*. This method of cleansing the internal body was the oldest way in the Kerala style of Ayurveda. Basically, medicated ghee given to you is supposed to go inside and aid cellular detoxification. This method of cleansing also impacted the mind and consciousness. I had the same dream patterns that I had at a Vipassana course and the Kushi Institute.

So in a nutshell, years later after a lot of reading on all three disciplines—Vipassana, macrobiotics and Ayurveda—the conclusion I have drawn has been this: Vipassana of course does have the ability to stir your consciousness at a very deep level. Therefore, any impurities that are in your unconscious mind will come to the surface in dreams and in sensations. However, in my current life, the path I chose was of becoming a macrobiotic food specialist. I have also successfully gone through several Ayurvedic *panchakarma* and *snehapanam* cleanses; these therapies touch one's consciousness on deep levels. In many ways, I am blessed to have encountered all these three disciplines in this life and I am using them together professionally and personally to help myself and others.

6

THE CAUSE OF SUFFERING AND KARMA: CAN WE AVOID IT?

Cause and Effect: 'Karma'

We know that our lives are a series of events, happenings, relationships and ups and downs; no matter how much money we have or not have, the one common denominator is death. While this statement sounds pessimistic, it's the truth. So in this big maze of life, the questions we must ask ourselves are these: Does suffering have a cause? If we can work towards removing the cause, can we, thus, end our suffering? In India, we have a term for the law of cause and effect: it's called *kamma*. The Buddha defined kamma as universal and fundamental to existence. The word karma (Sanskrit) is the same word, but popularly used to describe 'fate'. The two words have different connotations as fate is outside of us, beyond our control. Kamma on the other hand implies 'action', i.e., our own actions are the cause for whatever we experience. We are individually responsible for our actions. So, we can take our karma into our own hands and become masters of our so-called destiny. William Hart says:

> 'As it is each of us going through our lives are like a blindfolded man who has never learned to drive, sitting behind the wheels of a speeding car on a busy highway. We are not likely to reach our destination without a mishap. We may think we are driving the car, but actually the car is driving us. If we want to avoid an accident, we need to remove the blindfold, learn how to operate the vehicle and steer it out of danger as quickly as possible.'

He applies the same analogy to our lives where we must learn to perform actions that will lead us to where we really wish to go.[1]

It is important to understand action, in the context of kamma. There are three actions:

i. Physical
ii. Vocal
iii. Mental

According to the law of Dhamma, mental action is the most important of the three. Every action stems from the mental intention of that action first. The theory of karma is that every action bears some fruit which in turn contains the seed of more actions, which will also yield the appropriate fruit. Therefore, every arrow of action shot by the doer boomerangs, resulting in one of such arrows and the doer is caught up in the cycle of karma (action) and *phalam* (fruit). It becomes evident that it becomes impossible to escape from the fruits of one's actions. Thus, in order to break away from the vicious cycles of karma, one must have *control* over one's actions. For this, a thorough understanding of their generators, i.e., thoughts, is needed and thoughts have to be studied at their birthplace: the mind.

Nothing happens without a cause. Our intellect and senses cannot clearly find the cause, but there is always a cause. Our past actions give result to our current life and our current life will give result to our future. We do have control over present actions in order to change the future course of our life. The root cause of the problems we face lies in the mind of each individual and if each person starts to change, then society changes. The karmas of the past determine the flow of life we face and since we have the control of the present, we can change the flow of life in the future. You have no control over another, but do have full control of yourself.

What we Indians term as 'atma' or the 'soul' is nothing but that part of the mind that is reacting all the time, be it by craving or aversion for something or someone first coming up in the form of a sensation that a part of the mind terms as pleasant or unpleasant. We are attached to this part of the mind, and we give it a form called 'I', which we then get attached to with ego and we think it's a real person inside us—what we then term as 'a soul'. *Vipassana only addresses the truth happening within the framework of the body.* You have a physical body (matter) and the mind. When using the technique of Vipassana— as you keep moving from the gross to the subtle to the subtlest—i.e., you go to the tiniest subatomic particle that makes up your entire mind and matter structure which also arises and passes. This is not immortal. So where is the 'soul' that is considered immortal by any tradition? Beyond the framework—when and if you reach such a stage through the technique of meditation—you come to see that the mental structure is just energy in the form of wavelets arising and passing. This is when you can transcend mind and matter and here, in this state, nothing arises and passes—there is no material form, no mental form, no 'I'—and everyone has the ability to reach this stage. The entire universe is vibrating and is nothing but vibrations.

Nobody is the cause of your suffering but yourself. The technique of Vipassana works if one observes suffering objectively by sitting in meditation as taught through the technique. We cannot be attached to our suffering as we will not understand the cause of why we are unhappy. Human beings are ignorant and therefore generate sankharas (in Pali) and *samskara* (in Sanskrit) or mental dispositions formed volitionally.

Cause of Monkey Mind (Suffering)

The solution to the problem of suffering lies with us alone. Hence, we cannot blame anyone else for our actions. If we are miserable, we have sown the very seeds of misery first. It is after these seeds are sown that we create more misery around us. The wise people always say 'Know Thyself'. This is essentially the first step to get out of suffering. So, what makes up 'you'?

Matter

Know yourself not just on a superficial level, but on a deeper level. How can we do this? Let's try and understand this further. Beyond the physical form (your physical form), you are vaguely aware that inside you there is a fine-tuned machine; your organs working in harmony to give you good health. You also know the body has a set of biochemical reactions going on within each cell, which is what also makes you. Is this it? Not really. You are made of subatomic particles which have no real solidity: the life of these are much less than a trillionth of a second. These arise and pass in and out of existence, like a flow of vibrations. This is the ultimate reality of your being as discovered by the Buddha 2500 years ago. As explained in the previous chapter, while scientists have also accepted this theory on the human body as matter, it does not lead them to 'enlightenment' or an answer of what is the 'self'.

These subatomic particles are called *kalapas* (in Pali—the language of the Buddha—described as the smallest nano atoms we are made up of or invisible units so small that you cannot see) or *rupa kalapa* (comes from the Sanskrit *rupa* which means form and *kalapa* which means bundle). It describes the smallest unit of physical matter, said to be one-fourth the size of a particle of dust. These are composed of eight inseparable elements of material essence in varying amounts, which are earth, water, fire, air, smell, taste and nutrition. The first four (as mentioned) are called primary qualities and are predominant in kalapas. The other four are secondary properties that derive from primaries.[2] The very same kalapas that you are made of is what the entire material universe is made up of as well.

This is the ultimate reality of matter: a continual stream of waves or particles, what you term as 'myself'.[3]

Mind

Can we imagine our existence without our mind? I doubt it. While we are aware of how our conscious mind works, the realm of our unconscious mind is beyond our power of comprehension. Here is how the Vipassana technique looks at it.

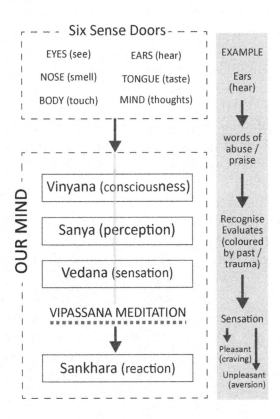

To understand consciousness, we must understand the four major segments of the mind: (1) *Vinyana*, which is consciousness. Its job is to cognize all the six sense doors: eyes, nose, body, tongue, ears and mind. These are six *vinyanas*. If a sound comes into contact with the ears, then the ears' consciousness will arise; if emotion comes into contact with the mind, the mind's consciousness will arise. So on and so forth, with a stimulus that comes into contact with each sense door. (2) *Sanya*, that is perception. Its job is to perceive a stimulus that comes into contact with any of the sense doors. For example, if words arise of abuse or praise, the sanya recognizes it as abuse or praise. (3) *Vedana* which experiences sensation as soon as an evaluation is given, let's say it's words of praise, there is a pleasant sensation which arises within the body, and it could be a subtle flow of pleasant sensations. Similarly, with words of abuse, there is a flow of unpleasant sensations on the body as the sanya has evaluated it as negative, i.e., abusive words. (4) *Sankhara* (reaction)—the motivation of the mind—it is a heap of 'action' and will respond with craving and aversion; the volition of the mind which results in mental action. There are three types of sankharas: one is like it's drawn on water, generated and gets eliminated. The second is like a line drawn on the sand and the third is like it's drawn on a rock: it is deep and takes years to eliminate. There is that stock of accumulated sankharas.

To understand consciousness further, let's step back a bit. Every moment within the framework of the body, masses of subatomic particles—*kalapas*—arise and pass away. How do they arise? The cause becomes clear as you investigate the reality as it is, without influence from any past conditioning or philosophical beliefs. The material input, the food that you have taken, becomes a cause for these kalapas to arise. You will also begin to understand that kalapas arise and pass due to the climatic atmosphere around you. In the Vipassana technique, you learn not only how these four parts of consciousness act out, but you also begin to understand the formation of the mind–matter structure: how mind helps matter to arise and dissolve. Every moment, depending on the food that is fed to the mind in thought (when your eyes are closed in meditation), a type of mind arises and the content of the mind, which determines the quality of the mind. For example, when a mind full of passion (or anger or fear) has arisen, you will notice that as it arises, it helps to generate these subatomic particles. Depending on what has arisen, let's say passion, with the material structure (mind), subatomic particles of a particular type arise and there is a biochemical secretion that starts flowing throughout the body with the bloodstream. In the case of passion—which the sanya evaluated—a sensual flow of sensations occurs. This affects the next moment of the mind, with more passion. Thus, a craving of passion starts at the mental level, which stimulates the sensual flow at the physical level. The behaviour pattern of the mind of continually generating the sankhara of passion is strengthened because of the repeated nature of this reaction. The nature of impurities of the mind, be it fear, anger, hatred, causing aversion; and lust, greed, passion, causing craving, are two polarities that the mind oscillates between. This habit pattern of the mind does not discriminate between religion, the nature of the mind applies to all. See illustration on page 71, which depicts our mind from a Vipassana standpoint.

As I mentioned, when I read books and tried to intellectualize this process—when Stephen Covey said 'proact' don't 'react', or Jiddu Krishnamurti said 'see things as they are'—I never understood how to actually do this or apply it to my life. I could not stop the cycle of craving or aversion. But when I went through my first Vipassana course, everything fell into place like the pieces of a big jigsaw puzzle. I knew how to do it finally: how I generated 'reaction' all the time and then acted it out.

The unconscious mind is actually not unconscious as it is in contact with the body and what it is going through at all times. A sensation is always arising and passing, arising and passing. This is because everything within the realm of your physical body has a charge: producing a sensation. There is a barrier between the conscious and unconscious minds. When you engage in Vipassana meditation, you break this barrier, while your surface-level mind keeps busy with outside objects or remains involved with games of intellectualization, imagination or emotion. You don't feel what's happening on the deeper levels of your mind and reactions that are taking place there.

For example, you are feeling a particular sensation which may be due to the food you have eaten, the atmosphere around you or due to your old mental reactions that are arising at the moment. Whatever it is, a sensation is always produced, and you keep reacting to it because of the old habit pattern of the mind. In Vipassana meditation, what we are trained to do is to observe this sensation (not judging it, or reacting to it), but with equanimity. When you sit for an hour of meditation, initially you will get a few moments of those 'non-reactive' states, but as your practice grows, those moments get extended and that's when you are changing the habit pattern of the mind. Vipassana teaches you how to experience those states of being in the now on an experiential level. This stops the habituated mind that reacts all the time. When at the deepest unconscious level the 'non-reaction' is felt, that's when a deep change happens. You start breaking a vicious cycle, the mind in reality was reacting to a sensation (chemically produced), but you were or have been engaged for hours battling through it. Now the mind gets a break from it, sometimes for a few seconds, a few minutes or for a whole hour. You soon come out of the misery of reaction. You have to experience this state and keep revisiting it, that's why meditation becomes important.

Let's Break It Down

We all know that there is someone or a voice that talks to us from within. Or at least we think we do. How does this voice that recognizes things around you, comprehend and take in stimuli and then think and make you decide what action to take? Something tells you what to do: you are tired now, sleep or call someone, makes you dream, make plans and so on. As you go along the journey of your life: dreaming, making plans, being attached to positive thoughts or negative ones, these are just a part of the 'monkey mind' playing its tricks on you. Your life exists largely beyond these thought processes, and also you are not in control. If you start analysing what you are really going through, it's a swing between two polarities: that of craving an outcome, i.e., something you want desperately to happen and aversion to something you'd like to move away from. While you feel your inner world is under your control, you are actually controlling that inner world and guiding it to experience craving or aversion . In reality, you are not reacting to stimuli in front of you but to the sensations your body produces.

Essentially, you see something or recreate an image of something in your mind. It produces a pleasant or an unpleasant sensation and you react to the sensation, not to the stimuli. This is something you do not know, simply because you do not experience this sensation. It just happens and the cognizing part of your mind—that which ascribes labels to everything—terms the sensation as pleasant or unpleasant and you react accordingly.

The ability to sharpen our 'awareness' to these sensations is the grey area, which is out of our control, where Vipassana comes in and helps, the *space* between a *stimulus* and a *response*. Once your mind is trained towards the 'awareness' of these sensations, it stops judging them as pleasant or unpleasant, but allows you to shift into the mode of the 'observer'. We all know that your chance to self-evolve lies in, as most people would say, controlling the 'mind', but only the great masters of meditation understand that it actually lies in not judging the sensations that are produced by the 'matter', your body, but by becoming an *observer* to them. Ask me: after all the spiritual reading I did, which in a gist, said that to attain true happiness, you must be an objective observer to your problems instead of getting lost in them; but no one teaches you how. Everyone intellectualizes it, but do they give you a path to follow? Yes, we have many New Age masters who have recycled all our yogic *kriyas* (breathing techniques) that aim at quietening the mind. But is this a permanent change in actually making you free from the sufferings that you feel embroil you all the time?

The Bhagavad Gita and Its Viewpoint

The Bhagavad Gita is a 700-verse Hindu scripture that is a part of the epic Mahabharata, attributed to sage Vyasa (more of a legend than a historical figure). The accepted dates are from the fifth century to the second century BCE (possibly the latter), as the possible time of these verses being put together. It is set in a narrative framework of a dialogue between Arjuna and his guide and charioteer Krishna (one of the most popular of the India divinities, worshipped as the eighth incarnation or avatar of the Hindu god Vishnu). I bring the Gita here and Krishna's role in the Mahabharata as his talks to Arjuna at the time of this battle are very similar to what the Buddha preached.[4] The Bhagavad Gita owes a lot of its wisdom to the Vedas, which are older than the Buddha (at least by 2500 years).[5]

I do not lean towards any form of doctrine here. Maybe some of you are thinking that if Vipassana is a secular technique then why am I bringing in the Gita? By highlighting what the Bhagavad Gita says on the subject,

I want to highlight the thinking that Indians are already steeped in, much before the subject of mindfulness came into practice in today's times. The Buddha lived in ancient India in the fifth to fourth century BCE. There are many similarities in what the Bhagavad Gita says and what the Buddha preached. Both emphasize the state of being a witness to one's life. The stress on observing your breath in meditation, given by Krishna to Arjuna, is the same as 'Anapana' meditation, i.e., the first part of Vipassana meditation.

If we try to digest properly the implications of the Bhagavad Gita's advice in the light of Indian Vedic lore, it becomes amply clear how actions performed without egocentric desires purge the mind of its deep-seated impressions and make it increasingly subtle in its purification and preparation for greater flights into the infinite beyond. The Gita goes on to explain: Mind is man; as the mind, so is the individual. If the mind is disturbed, the individual is disturbed. If the mind is good, the individual is good. The mind is constituted of two distinct sides: one facing the world of stimuli that reach it from *outside* objects of the world and the other, facing *within* which reacts to the stimuli received. The outer mind facing the object is called the objective mind—in Sanskrit we call it *manas*—and the inner mind is called the subjective mind—in Sanskrit, the *buddhi*.

The Gita says the individual is whole and healthy in whom the objective and subjective aspects of the mind work in unison with each other and in moments of doubt, the objective mind readily comes under the disciplining influence of the subjective mind. But unfortunately, except for a rare few, the majority of us have minds that are split. The split—between the subjective and the objective aspects of the mind—is mainly created by the layer of egoistic desires in the individual. The greater the distance between these two phases of the mind, the greater the inner confusion in the individual and the greater the egoism and low desires which the individual comes to exhibit in life.

Through the five 'gateways of knowledge', the organs of perception, all of us experience the world of objects around us at all moments of our waking state. The innumerable stimuli that react with our sense organs (receptors) create impulses which reach the objective mind and these impulses filter deep down to the subjective stratum through the intervening layers of individual egocentric desires (I can assume here, by egocentric desires, what the Bhagavad Gita is advocating is past conditioning, attachment to the self, life's experiences). With these impulses—thus reaching the subjective mind of a person—each person reacts with existing impressions of his/her own past actions that are carefully stored away in the subjective layer and express themselves in the world through the five organs of action.

At each moment, we human beings meet with different patterns of these stimuli and thus constantly gather new information and impressions in the 'subjective mind'. This is the part of the mind that is coloured with our own prejudices. Every set of impulses reaching it not only adds to the existing layers of impressions already in it, but also gets coloured by the quality of these *vasanas* hoarded within. Let's define this term here itself. Vasanas are unmanifested

desires, e.g., a man who loves art is asleep at night when
nothing happens to these desires; the state of desires in deep
sleep are vasanas when they are not manifesting. The state
of unmanifested desires are the ones that will manifest into
desires eventually and then into action. Vasanas are the
root of everything about our lives. You had a vasana for
philosophy, so you had a thought in your head and you are
listening to a philosophical talk (action). Vasanas are the
cause of everything about us. They are also called the bliss
sheath, where no thoughts are expressed or manifested
and we experience a calmness and bliss. Also known as
'ignorance', our whole personality and all our world arises
because of the ignorance of the self, so vasanas are ignorance
of the self. Since we do not know ourselves, we have a
personality and a world; once we gain the knowledge of the
self, both personality and world will cease to exist.[6] When
these vasanas are translated into action, the actions carry a
flavour of the existing vasanas in the subjective mind.

Man is not aware of what he can be or do, when
the subjective mind is cleared of Vasanas gathered by
its egocentric, passionate existence in the world. In the
Bhagavad Gita, it is said:

> When I look into a mirror and do not see my face
> in it, it is not because the mirror is not reflecting the
> object in front of it, but because the reflected image
> is not perceptible to my vision due to, perhaps, the
> thick layer of dust on the mirror. With a duster, when I
> clean the mirror, the act of cleaning does not create the
> reflection of the face, but it only unveils the reflection
> which was already there.[7]

The Gita says that we need to bring both the objective mind and the subjective mind together into a happy marriage, where the objective mind is well disciplined to act faithfully as per the guidance of the subjective mind. This is only accomplished by the removal of the dividing factor: egocentric desires. It is then that a yogi or yogini becomes skilled in action. It is then that this person reacts intelligently and faithfully with the objective mind to external stimuli. Their actions become, as it were, a purgation of the already existing vasanas in their subjective mind.

The question is, how do we do this? In the Gita, it is emphasized that we must use 'selfless activity'— performed in a state of egoless adoration and reverence to the divine ideal—that would ultimately result in inner purification. This, the Gita says, is a prerequisite for the subjective mind to reach some sort of harmony. However, if we ask ourselves the truthful question—as to whether this is actually possible—we will come up with only one answer: not really. With all due respect to the Bhagavad Gita—while it has put forth concepts very brilliantly for us to follow—it still intellectualizes them like most other spiritual texts do, but there is no means of 'experiencing' this state and actually eradicating that which is stored in our subjective mind. An average person can read this and try to be selfless or follow a path of bhakti, but how does he/she reach the unmanifested vasanas coloured by past conditionings, attachments to certain patterns we recreate and the new stock that we keep creating on a daily basis? The tragedy is that an average person is ignorant that this sort of distinction even exists (I say this with respect to all those reading this book). The subjective mind is spiritually viewed by the Bhagavad Gita as a secret weapon in us human beings to be used as an outlet for existing impressions that have come to be stored in it. Human beings misuse this dangerous weapon and bring about their own downfall, when they use it as an inlet and act out during their supposedly selfish activities, which they perform with motives and feelings of attachment, multiplying and adding a new stock of mental impressions. In order for us to exhaust these, nature provides us with a new body, in which the same ego comes to live, repeatedly, life after life. By ego here, the Bhagavad Gita points to 'flow of consciousness' that carries on till we exhaust the deep realms of our mind of all impressions.

7

WHO ARE YOU?

Who Are You in Reality?

In his book *Who Am I* by Ramana Maharshi[1], a set of question and answers expounds this inquiry. Here he says:

> All living beings desire to be happy always, without any misery. In everyone there is observed supreme love for oneself. And happiness alone is the cause of love. In order therefore, to gain that happiness which is one's nature and which is experienced in the state of deep sleep, where there is no mind, one should know oneself. To achieve this, the Path of Knowledge, the enquiry in the form of 'Who am I?', is the principal means.

If the above analogy is extended and we were to look at a 'no mind' state, then deep states of meditation also take you to this state of no mind. He further goes on to qualify what 'I am not'. (By this he means, 'What you are not.')

This is where the above explanation of how the technique of Vipassana works also comes into play, including what I have explained earlier, that you are made up of mere vibrations arising. Technically, you are not this body that you are attached to or even your mind. Ramana Maharshi says:

> The gross body is composed of seven humours (*dhatus*), I am not; the five cognitive sense organs, viz., the sense of hearing, touch, sight, taste and smell, which apprehend their respective objects, viz., sound, touch, colour, taste and odour, I am not; the five cognitive sense organs, viz., the organs of speech, locomotion, grasping, excretion and procreation, which have as their respective functions, speaking, moving, grasping, excreting and enjoying, I am not; the vital airs, prana, etc., I am not; even the mind which thinks, I am not; the nescience [lack of knowledge or awareness] too, which is endowed only with the residual impressions of objects and in which there are no objects and no functioning I am not. If I am none of these, then who am I? After negating all of the above mentioned as 'not this', 'not this,' that Awareness which alone remains— that I am.

In one of the last questions, he gives the distinction between inquiry and meditation. Inquiry consists in retaining the mind in the Self. Meditation consists in thinking that one's self is *Brahman, Existence–Consciousness–Bliss*.

When I was a so-called 'spiritual seeker'—reading all the books I could lay my hands on—I thought 'enlightenment' or 'self-realization' was a place to reach and it could be done quickly. I also thought if I did get 'enlightened' I would be Wonder Woman. But I was wrong. As I mentioned earlier, I first understood stuff on an intellectual level. Then when I started practicing Vipassana meditation, I started experiencing mind and matter and the constant fight between the two. The Buddha keeps saying that enlightenment meant the end of suffering. *So, when I started seeing that suffering was a part of what I created—the seed of all suffering started with me—I realized that only I had the power to change this slowly but surely.* While doing Vipassana, I realized that what we Hindus call a soul is just a reacting mind, a certain part of the mind. Yet I was always ascribing an 'I' to this reacting mind; this illusion of 'I' just drops when you practice Vipassana. It became apparent that Vipassana was nothing but the investigation of what was going on within the framework of the body which would lead me to the truth. One first encounters the gross body (that is the physical body) and then the subtler body, and when we engage in Vipassana, we come to understand that all we are is vibrations. When you actually experience the arising and passing of these vibrations (within your mind and matter framework) there are moments after many years of practice for some, while it comes sooner for others, where you transcend the field of mind and matter where nothing arises or passes away. Some may term it as being immortal, but here there is no sense of 'I'. This is a stage we have to experience ourselves, to believe 'Who are we' or define 'Who am I'.

'Suffering', that which makes us unhappy or being 'elated', are just two sides of a coin that we cannot take seriously as they come out of mere attachments to sensations that our mind judges as bad and good. Vipassana focuses on being equanimous to both types of polarities: the good and the bad sensations (they are actually the same). To be happy, we must strive for this kind of equanimity. The key to practicing Vipassana lies in *accepting*.

What Is Your Destiny and Your Role?

Destiny is quite literally in your hands. Our past actions cannot be changed and this guides the flow of life. According to our past actions (karma) which only we have created, they will guide what we attract in our present. What we change is our reaction and the subsequent action to these sensations that we give into. The truth really is that we are the masters of our own destiny. Karma and destiny are intertwined. If we master our mind, we master our destiny. When S.N. Goenka says it all starts with the breath and observing it—natural, normal breath—it seems the most simplistic way to come out of misery. Yet, it is the absolute truth and in my experience the only way to be a better person as well. Observing the breath, then the sensations, which we are constantly reacting to— with craving or aversion—we generate negativity or an attachment. The truth is while we think there is an inner soul or some entity within us guiding everything we do, the reality is that there is no such entity. The Buddha said, 'Events happen, deeds are done, but there is no individual doer thereof'. As Ramesh Balsekar[2] explains it:

So now the question is, is it possible at all to give up the sense of personal doership so that one can be anchored in the experience of 'the end of suffering' while facing life from moment to moment? The answer, of course, is yes, it can be done because there have been people who have been accepted by the world as 'sages' who have indeed been actual examples of individuals for whom 'the end of suffering' has happened. What we see is that these sages live from moment to moment, enjoying the same pleasures and suffering the same kind of pains that the ordinary person is subjected to, but anchored in peace and harmony.

Crossing the Threshold of Negativity

How should you get over suffering and just learn how to be a kind person or someone who is not destructive to oneself or others? This can be a very 'esoteric' way of looking at negativity. But let's take the most extreme acting out of negativity, that of when one commits a crime. A film called *Doing Time, Doing Vipassana* depicts the whole process of this really well. It shows us how Vipassana was introduced to Tihar jail by Kiran Bedi, then IG Prisons, who was trying to reform inmates in the jail. It was a very bold step. She was trying to find a solution to the prisoners' emotional problems. On 4 April 1994, 1,003 male prisoners gathered to attend a course that was inaugurated by S.N. Goenka, with courses introduced for female prisoners as well.

Later on, two scientific studies were carried out to assess the impact of Vipassana on the prisoners' mental health. The dimensions studied were well-being, hostility, hope, helplessness, personality, psychopathy—and in the case of psychiatric disorders—anxiety and depression. The first study consisted of a group of 120 random prisoners selected from a list of 300 (conducted in January 1994), while the second study was conducted with 150 prisoners. There were control groups and experimental groups set up in both studies. The control group comprised of prisoners who had not attended a ten-day Vipassana course and the experimental group comprised of those who attended the course. All subjects were assessed before, immediately after and three months after the course. They were assessed with the help of scientifically valid psychological testing and clinical interviews by a team of five, including psychologists, psychiatrists and social workers. In the first study, a six-month follow-up was also carried out.

Conclusion

Immediately after the course, the experimental group subjects were found to be less hostile towards their environment and felt less helpless. Subjects without any psychological symptoms also reported improvement in the form of enhanced well-being and a sense of hope for the future.

Our lives throw at us many situations that we cannot deal with. Recently, I lost my mother—it happened while I was writing this book. I remember describing to a friend what I was going through, the grieving process after losing her. I felt as if someone had cut my legs off.

Then, at another time, I caught myself telling another friend, I felt my heart had been pulled out of my body. I have gone through anger, blame (directed at the medical system), despair, loneliness, helplessness like I have never experienced before. The pain of losing someone so dear to you is unbearable. All of us go through some kind of pain like this at some point or another in our lives. Stewing in it is not the answer. The only sane thing I have done through this span is sit for my meditation practice daily for an hour at least. It has given me the strength to deal with the pain, process it and move on.

PART TWO

8

HISTORY OF VIPASSANA

Story of the Buddha: Where Did It All Begin?

The Buddha means the awakened or enlightened one (also known as Siddhartha Gautama, he was a prince turned philosopher, religious leader and meditator living in India c. 563 BCE to 483 BCE). While he is the founder of Buddhism, one of the most important gifts he gave to India is the technique of meditation he used to gain enlightenment, called Vipassana. He taught this meditation for forty-five years till he passed away.

Vipassana means 'to see things as they really are': the meditation itself is a non-sectarian technique and seeks to eradicate mental impurities. Vipassana is a method of meditation used for self-transformation through self-observation. It focuses on the deep interconnection between mind and body, which can be experienced directly by disciplined attention to the physical sensations that form the life of the body and that continuously interconnect and condition the life of the mind. It is this observation-based, self-exploratory journey to the common root of mind and body that dissolves mental impurity, resulting in a balanced mind full of love and compassion.

Since the time of the Buddha, Vipassana has been handed down to the present day by an unbroken chain of teachers. Although Indian by descent, Satya Narayan Goenka, who passed away in 2013 at the age of eighty-nine, was born and raised in Burma (Myanmar). While living there, he had the good fortune to learn Vipassana from his teacher, Sayagyi U Ba Khin, who at the time was a high-ranking government official. S.N. Goenka studied under his teacher for fourteen years before he brought the technique to India in 1969.

Over a period of forty-five years, S.N. Goenka and the teachers appointed by him taught hundreds of thousands of people in courses in India and other countries, east and west. Vipassana has spread all over the world and is being taught to people of all races, sects and religions.

The technique taught by S.N. Goenka goes back two-and-a-half millennia to the Buddha. The Buddha never taught a sectarian religion; he taught Dhamma or Dharma (in Pali) which means the law of nature or the truth and the way to liberation, which is universal. S.N. Goenka retained the purity of this technique, i.e., the way it was taught by the Buddha.

S.N. Goenka was the recipient of many awards and honours in his lifetime including the prestigious Padma Bhushan—the highest civilian award given by the Indian President—in 2012.

Despite having brought such a great gem back to India and then have had it spread from India to the rest of the world—when you visit a Vipassana centre, there is no big statue or picture that lets you know he was instrumental in this process. As a civilization, India's largest achievement is its history. That's what makes disciplines like Ayurveda, Vipassana or yoga steeped in their beginnings—what the Western world came to terms with much later on. I again don't mean this as a comment that should make India sound superior, but India has definitely given to the world some practices—which the West just uses as a basis to validate their systems—centuries ago.

So, while the history of Vipassana was rediscovered by the Buddha 2500 years ago, S.N. Goenka needs a mention in its history for having reintroduced it to India. Here is his story.

Shri Satya Narayan Goenka

Born in 1924 in Burma (now Myanmar) to Indian parents from the Marwari community, S.N. Goenka grew up in a conservative Hindu household. He was a successful businessman and started experiencing severe migraines. Even though he was on medication, he found no relief. He used to narrate his story on finishing the first ten-day course and very lovingly, he said he was blessed to be born into a business family, so he knew what it was like to have the money and still not be happy. He was a leader of the Hindu community and gave a lot of talks on Hindu religious texts. It was when he was prescribed morphine by his doctors to get relief from his migraines, that he soon became addicted to it. Now he needed a treatment to get out of his morphine dependency.

In 1955, a friend suggested he visit the Vipassana centre headed by Sayagyi U Ba Khin who was a civil servant and Vipassana teacher. He said that when he met Sayagyi U Ba Khin, he told him that he came to get rid of his headaches after which Sayagyi U Ba Khin told him he should return to his home. He further explained to him that Vipassana is a technique to overcome the impurities in the mind and if he decides to stay on, then this is the 'intent' he must have to learn this technique. If in the bargain his headaches were to go, then this was an added bonus, as they were a by-product of the mind's impurities, Sayagyi U Ba Khin told S.N. Goenka. This is what made S.N. Goenka stay on at the centre.

On learning Vipassana from Sayagyi U Ba Khin, S.N. Goenka found a discipline that went far beyond alleviating the symptoms of physical disease which transcended cultural and religious barriers. Vipassana gradually transformed his life in the ensuing years of practice and study under the guidance of his teacher.

In 1969, S.N. Goenka was authorized as a Vipassana meditation teacher by Sayagyi U Ba Khin. He first came to India to teach meditation to his parents and some close relatives. After he taught them the course, some relatives asked him to conduct another one in their village. After this, he left his business to his family and moved to India, where he began to reintroduce Vipassana. The first Vipassana meditation space was in Hyderabad. Seven years later, in 1976, he opened his first meditation centre,

Dhamma Giri in Igatpuri near Nashik in Maharashtra. This is where I have done all my twenty-three courses. He taught meditation on his own till 1982, when he started training teachers in the technique. I have attended one course where he sat in on all our morning meditations in 1996. Up until 1998, he frequented this campus, where I got to meet him on his morning walks and attend question and answer sessions which took place at his residence at Dhamma Giri.

Mr Goenka used all his business genius to give back to India a standardized course which is now run in 341 locations across ninety-four countries, with seventy-eight of these locations in India. I also attended the establishing of the Global Vipassana Pagoda at Gorai Beach in Mumbai, built as a tribute to his teacher who in turn felt he had to pay his debt back to India, the land of the origin of Vipassana.

The qualities that Vipassana upholds run through the fabric of the teachers and starts with Mr Goenka as the entity who started it. He was the most pragmatic, sweet, happy and generous man in spirit you could have ever known. He was strong like a lion, with a powerful voice and conscious minute-to-minute and had the calmness of a mind that was razor-sharp. Compassion overflowed from his heart, for him all were equal. In his discourses, he was full of humour and always made you laugh at the end of a hard day's meditation and emotional upheaval; his discourses felt like a balm after just one day at a course.

Despite his magnetic presence, S.N. Goenka had no wish to be a guru who turns his disciples into automatons. Instead, he taught self-responsibility. The real test of

Vipassana, he said, was applying it in life. He encouraged meditators not to sit at his feet, but to go out and live happily in the world. He shunned all expressions of devotion to him, instead directing his students to be devoted to the technique, to the truth that they find within themselves.

To maintain its purity, S.N. Goenka never made the teaching of the technique of Vipassana meditation a business. Courses and centres operating under his direction are all run on a totally non-profit basis. Each course runs on the donations of students that complete the course. Teachers are not on a payroll, neither are those who work in administration at a Vipassana centre. Services by individuals are voluntary, except for those from the staff—running day-to-day operations like cleaning or cooking, etc.—who get paid. He has reintroduced this technique as a service to humanity and it has continued to run in the same fashion since its inception.

Vipassana has never been publicized. Even though S.N. Goenka was invited as a speaker to the Millennium World Peace Summit of Religious and Spiritual Leaders in 2000 and was awarded the Padma Bhushan in 2012, we never heard of it unless one looked it up as research. He has trained 1300 teachers in the technique of Vipassana. Approximately 1,20,000 people attend courses every year. Jack Kornfield (American author and teacher in the Vipassana movement in American Theravada Buddhism) said, on the death of S.N. Goenka:

In every generation, there are a few visionary and profound masters who hold high the lamp of the

Dharma to illuminate the world. Like the Dalai Lama and Thich Nhat Hanh, Ven. S.N. Goenka was one of the great world masters of our time.

Jay Michaelson[1] described him as follows:

> He was a core teacher for the first generation of 'insight' meditation teachers to have an impact in the United States. He emphasized that meditation was not spirituality and not religion, but more like a technology—a set of tools for upgrading and optimizing the mind.

In all my years growing up—before I landed up at Dhamma Giri to do my course—I read all the big gurus on using mind strategies for success in life: Daniel Goleman (*Emotional Intelligence,* the one book that made sense to me), Stephen Covey (7 *Habits of Highly Effective People.* Message: be proactive, not reactive) and Anthony Robbins (*Unlimited Power, Giant Steps, Inner Strength*). These remained strategies and sooner or later nothing went within to tackle the issues the mind would come up with. When I went through just one ten-day course, as I mentioned earlier, all that spiritual reading and all these books made sense. I finally had experienced what lies within the field of matter and mind, to know what created the problems on my mind level. I agree with Michaelson when he says that, for S.N. Goenka, '. . . meditation was not spirituality and not religion, but more like a technology, a set of tools for upgrading and optimizing the mind.' The first victory was what I felt on a mind-strategy front. I never needed to strategize any more: I knew now why and how to act from a centre far deeper than just the mind.

Mr Goenka's legacy was just too huge for humankind to bear and fathom. What this one person has done for us is a way to create what my macrobiotics teacher Michio Kushi embraced of 'One Peaceful World'. This was the one tool we could all use to come out happier, kinder, more compassionate and loving people.

9

LIVING YOUR LIFE AND SHAPING YOUR WORLD VIEW

'The fact of the matter is that all apparent forms of matter and body are momentary clusters of energy. We are little more than flickers on a multidimensional television screen. This realization directly experienced can be delightful. You suddenly wake up from the delusion of separate form and hook up to the cosmic dance.'

—Timothy Leary[1]

Life's Little Lessons

The following chapters—for most people who have done a Vipassana course—will seem a bit odd, as we—I don't say 'we' with any sort of judgement, but more because 'we' implies me and you who have done a Vipassana course—have done it to understand how easy it becomes to practise what I am about to enumerate. I also felt that—while I was continuing my meditation practice—I also read a lot and this helped me arrive at some simple tenets on my journey to become whole again (still striving, I say this with no ego) that perhaps you could start thinking about. I have focused on these all through my life and they have worked for me, along with my meditation practice, to fix all that was broken in my life.

The technique of Vipassana meditation starts changing the basic habit pattern of the mind. Naturally if it changes the habit pattern of the mind and results in you as an individual generating close to no negativity on any level, then it is bound to not only affect your nature in a positive way, but also make you focus on attracting what you want in life. I am very fortunate that both the macrobiotic approach and Vipassana achieve the same results. The macrobiotic approach makes one eat clean, to keep the blood condition clean and if that happens, then energetically (by this I mean your own 'vibrational' level) one is beating to a different rhythm. The same holds true of Vipassana because as one has changed the intrinsic nature of the mind (that is to react all the time); one starts creating moments of only positivity.

I have lived the life after starting Vipassana and practicing macrobiotics and I don't need any study to validate the fact that Vipassana meditation changes you in ways that you yourself will sometimes not be able to define. Meditation is the new medicine. Vipassana meditation will not just change you—by this I mean take you away from the negative spaces in your head—but also impact you on a physical level by decreasing stress, increasing productivity, helping you to sleep better, relieving anxiety, improving immune function and also increasing performance. It will also help you (and I say this as do many other meditation practitioners) to manifest things in your life that you want without any craving for them, that is, without being attached to them in a crazy way.

We are attached to outcomes. Even if we pray, we pray for things, material or non-material. When you engage in a technique like Vipassana, you start changing the basic pattern of the way you think and see your reality and because you manage to do this with great success, life on a day-to-day basis becomes easy to deal with. For this, I might need to lean on the way quantum physics puts forth its view, only because it validates the Vipassana meditation framework. How can the mind affect tangible things in our lives?

As explained earlier, if everything in the universe is just made up of subatomic particles and are in a wave state while they are not being observed, they are potentially 'everything' and 'nothing' until they are observed. They exist everywhere and nowhere until they are observed. Thus, everything in our physical reality exists as pure potential.[2] This simply also means that you can create anything you want in the future for yourself as, if you give it enough energy, you can manifest it. All the qualities you hold as an ideal version of yourself, if you think it and give it enough energy, you can be that version of yourself. Your consciousness has an effect on energy around you. This is because your consciousness is also simply energy. As Joe Dispenza puts it, 'You are powerful enough to influence matter because at the most elementary level, you are energy with a consciousness. You are mindful matter'.

Our mode of communication with the universe is through our thoughts and feelings. Dispenza describes thoughts as the electrical charge in the quantum field and feelings as the magnetic charge in the field. The thoughts we think send an electrical signal out into the field. The feeling we generate magnetically draws events back to us. This should prompt us to ask, 'What am I broadcasting (consciously or unconsciously) on a daily basis?'

For a minute I am taking you away from the Vipassana meditation technique itself to simply make you think out of the box about your life and how you can influence it, why you must seize the day and take life into your own hands. If we have to become this person, it means we have to rise above all the petty stuff we hang on to. We cannot be the same person—with the same negative behaviour patterns—and not try to break away from that negative mould.

Vipassana is your way to bridge this gap between what you are and what you can potentially become. Meditation will start changing your thoughts, feelings and the natural outcome of all behaviour patterns. To align your thoughts, you have to experience the mind and matter (body) doing their song and dance and then come to a deep 'real' understanding—not just an intellectual understanding—of what makes you tick.

As explained earlier, we are made up of the same elements that the universe is made up of. The body is made up of (your atoms, sub-atoms) space, earth, water, fire and air. Even Ayurveda talks about the seven dhatus (plasma, blood, muscle, fat, bone, bone marrow and reproductive fluid) being dominated by these elements:

space, earth, water, fire and air.[3] The quantum field or the universe is also made up of the same elements, which form the basis of all material creation. The Vedas (religious texts of ancient India) described them as the *Pancha Maha Bhutas*, the fundamental building blocks of the Universe. So, what I am trying to get through to you is that we as human beings are made up of the same energy that exists outside of us. Dispenza puts forth this idea lucidly, also concluding that our physiological vehicle is made up of the same stuff as the rest of the universe. He says energy waves carry information and it makes sense to refer to the quantum field as an 'invisible intelligence':

> Think of the preceding conversation as a kind of template for how this intelligence has constructed reality. The quantum field is invisible potential energy that is able to organize itself from energy to subatomic particles to atoms to molecules and on up the line to everything. From a physiological perspective, it organizes molecules into cells into tissues into organs into systems and finally into the body as a whole. Put another way, this potential energy lowers itself as a frequency of wave patterns until it appears solid. It is this universal intelligence that gives life to that field and everything in it, including you and me. This power is the same universal mind that animates every aspect of the material universe. This intelligence keeps our hearts beating and our stomachs digesting food and oversees an incalculable number of chemical reactions per second that take place in every cell. Moreover, the

same consciousness prompts trees to grow fruit and causes distant galaxies to form and collapse. Because it exists in all places and times and exerts its power within us and all around us, this intelligence is both personal and universal.[4]

This is what Dispenza calls universal intelligence (Buddha calls it 'flow of consciousness').

Accept Responsibility

We are the cause of everything that happens in our life if, as explained earlier, you are the one reacting to stimuli constantly through your own coloured lenses of past conditionings, tribal rules (by this I mean what sort of an environment you grew up in and what kind of rules your family imposed upon you) and social factors. I would also add here: the stock of past *karmas* that you have carried over. Some of you may believe this after having read the previous chapters, while others may not. But please read on anyway as you will take away something from this section.

As I have gone through my life—just as you have yours—you will come to understand that there are many situations you will find yourself in that have really no explanation at all. We all know that we react to those that are negative with more ferocity. The negative things that happen to us, the misery they put us through, is because of our reaction not to 'them'—say a person or situation—but by actually attracting these situations, because of our own judgement of a reaction to the sensation produced within our bodies (matter). I think I have hammered this point in enough by now.

A growing body of research shows that emotional rigidity—getting hooked by thoughts, feelings and behaviours that don't serve us—is associated with a range of psychological skills, including emotional agility. Being flexible with your thoughts and feelings so that you can respond optimally to everyday situations is key to well-being and success.

Emotional agility is about loosening up, calming down and living with more intention. It's about choosing how you will respond to your emotional warning system. It supports the approach described by Viktor Frankl, the psychiatrist who survived a Nazi death camp and went on to write *Man's Search for Meaning*, a book on leading a more meaningful life in which our human potential can be fulfilled:

> Between stimulus and response there is a space. In that space is our power to choose our response. In our response lies our growth and our freedom.[5]

Vipassana, as I mentioned earlier, helps you tap into this space and transform through accessing it. By opening up the space between how you feel and what you should do about those feelings, emotional agility has been shown to help people with any number of troubles: negative self-image, heartbreak, physical pain, anxiety, depression, procrastination, tough transitions and more. Emotionally agile people are able to tolerate high levels of stress and endure setbacks, while remaining engaged, open and receptive. They do experience feelings of anger and sadness, but they face these with curiosity, self-compassion and acceptance. And rather than letting these feelings derail them, emotionally agile people effectively turn themselves—warts and all—towards their loftiest ambitions.

'The world is movement, and you cannot be stationary in your attitude towards something that is moving.'

—Henri Cartier-Bresson[6]

So, if this is indeed the case, then should we not just remain equanimous and 'accept responsibility' of our own reactions or judgements? Eckhart Tolle illuminates this very well when asked the question: If you call some emotions as negative, aren't you creating a mental polarity of good and bad? His answer: 'No. The polarity was created at an earlier stage when your mind judged the present moment as bad; this judgement then created the negative emotion.'[7]

When we accept our emotions as arising within us and we are creating them, we realize giving vent to them verbally, in thought or even physically is of no use. If you observe these and start engaging in Vipassana meditation (see things for what they are and access the 'space' between stimulus and reaction)—first by observing the breath (Anapana meditation) then engaging in Vipassana meditation—you will transmute the moment of reaction and move to the next stage. In separation of yourself from your non-acceptance is an attachment to a false sense of ego. Once you take full responsibility of your feelings, then you redeem yourself and actually are no longer tied to the negativity that they will produce from you.

Let me take you through my own story: when I was married and my ex-husband chose to engage in drama (his own and I, again, say this with no judgement), my tendency initially was to react and get involved with every stimulus he threw in my direction. However, after I attended my first course, I learnt how to access the space between a stimulus and response. So when there was a stimulus that in the past would make me react to him, I would now observe my quickening breath or even heat generated (basically anger, manifested in bodily sensations) at my extremities. I did not label this heat as good or bad, just observed it; in doing this I would not react. This made me hit another level of my own consciousness and is something I chose to do. I accepted responsibility of my own enactment of anger acting outward. This did not mean I bottled myself up with emotions. I simply decided to observe what came over me in sensations and how my breath responded to the stimuli around (could have been hateful words, loud music at 3 a.m., bad language); I remained steady. So I 'accepted responsibility' of myself. S.N. Goenka, in one of his discourses, said if someone chose to bring you 'gifts' (of bad language or behaviour that was negative) you always have the choice of returning them by not accepting them. This is exactly how I got in those heated moments.

Move On

We often fall into a victim mode in our lives. When something happens to us, we tend to fall into this mode of 'why me' more easily than another mode which could say 'why not me.' When I decided to quit my marriage, it was a very conscious decision. I had given my marriage eight and a half years. I knew what lay ahead of me was not going to be easy. Once I would announce my need for a divorce, my ex-husband would not let go of the marriage easily and would fight it in the divorce courts. I would be left penniless for a while and it was going to be an uphill task. Before Vipassana came into my life, I always played the victim card. Eckhart Tolle explains this in a way that you can understand what he calls the 'pain-body'. He says as long as you don't live in the 'now', you are attached to your 'pain-body' which surfaces from time to time. The pain-body is dormant most times (90 per cent of the time) in people who are of generally happy dispositions. However, if you are deeply unhappy, then it's active most times (the reverse 90 per cent of the time). Some people live through their pain-bodies while some experience this pain-body in certain situations. Anything can trigger it, and it's usually associated with patterns of your past. The pain-body survives if you identify with it, it becomes you when you give it attention.

I lived through my pain-body till I encountered Vipassana. Therefore, I had the ability to now disassociate myself from it and 'move on'. I remember sitting my in-laws down and having a chat with them and telling them I forgave them for what had happened in my marriage, but it was time I called it quits. They were most calm because I was calm. They knew I was serious and had made up my mind. It took a lot of guts to talk to the very people who had caused me so much anguish and pain with so much love and forgiveness.

I attribute this to my courses at Vipassana and the many hours of meditation. It took me eight and a half years to call it quits and finally move on.

The pain-body is cast by the ego and is actually afraid of the light of your consciousness. It is afraid of being found out. Its survival depends on your unconscious identification with it as well as on your unconscious fear of facing the pain that lives in you. But if you don't face it, if you don't bring the light of your consciousness into the pain, you will be forced to relive it again and again. The pain-body may seem to you like a dangerous monster that you cannot bear to look at, but I assure you that it is an insubstantial phantom that cannot prevail against the power of your presence.[8]

One way I had accessed what this light of consciousness was, was through Vipassana meditation, and I carried this into the discussion I had with my in-laws before walking away. All the angst you build up in any situation in life is simply that: just building it all up, attaching to your pain-body. In retrospect, after being on this path of Vipassana, I have come to realize that every situation in life is simply an attachment to your ego and the many pain-bodies you have accumulated. The missing link is having a technique that can help you shake it all off. Disassociate with yourself, because in reality there is no 'self'. This, then, brings you to the present moment: it's just your mind and matter playing tricks with you all the time. If you get a chance to work through this dance, you open yourself to a higher energy that works for you, creating 'space', the space to actually 'move on' with a lot of love from any situation.

Reclaim Your Mind Space

I remember when I finally spoke my decision out of wanting to move on from my marriage, I created 'space'. By this, I mean the burden of everything lifted from my being. I sat and had a cup of tea at my window and just stared into the green palms in my garden. Finally, what Jiddu Krishnamurti meant when he said 'see things as they really are', made sense. I was just observing the palm trees. I did not see how beautiful they looked or crave the sensation of prolonging the moment. I was so still and so present that I did not even realize how long I must have sat there: I was just in the now. I had finally 'reclaimed my space'. By this I mean, my mind space. Caroline Myss, a medical intuitive (an alternative medical practitioner who claims to use their self-described intuitive abilities to find the cause of a physical or emotional condition, through the use of insight rather than modern medicine), talks about 'calling your spirit back' in her book *Anatomy of the Spirit*. She basically explains how life's experiences can drain us and our life force and capture our spirit or power. Yet, we can transcend any situation to call back the power that has been taken from us. We can call our power back in various ways and meditation happens to be one of the ways in which we do this.[9] Of course the words 'spirit' or 'energy' are used interchangeably and simply mean that you can always reclaim your space. The choice is yours and yours alone.

I could have fallen into a deep depression with what I had gone through. God knows there were many times I wanted to run away to a place where I was not known.

I never thought about ending my life, no: I am not a quitter. Perhaps the positivity of a great upbringing and my parents, who had gone through Partition, had inculcated a resolve buried deep in my DNA and made it a sane and also the most nurturing childhood. But, I feel that to 'reclaim your life', you cannot escape again, so while self-help books may tell you to do stuff to escape your situation, like travel, talk to your psychologist (this helps up to a point, sure), declutter your space, try something new, rest or even change negative conversations, etc., there is nothing like reconnecting with your breath, the bridge between the body (matter) and your mind. In the stillness of this space, you will find over time (after meditating again and again and again . . . and sticking to it), the ability to reclaim your mind space and your life.

Create Space for Grace

If I had a daughter, I would have named her Grace. Growing up, I was super aggressive. This came from all the unresolved anger I had towards my father, whose rules for being the firstborn girl were totally different than for my younger brother. I had to come home early at 6 p.m. after playing with my friends: he called it curfew. My brother's curfew was not defined. As far as I can remember—when I opened my eyes to being all grown up—I had a voice, but couldn't use it at the dinner table, which was another rule he imposed. He did not like arguments. I used to be shooed away (this is how I remember it) to my room. This does not take away from the fact that he was my biggest teacher in life and one of the softest, but also angriest men

I knew. This was because of what he went through as a kid post-Partition, with his parents gone and him (at the age of eleven) being split from his older brother and sent to his sister's place to be brought up. Bottom line, I grew up angry: now that I look back, it was so silly. But, I think this is the one sankhara or karma I worked out through Vipassana. S.N. Goenka (as mentioned earlier) said we have some karmas that are like a line drawn in a rock: this was mine. Today I am the opposite: sure, I burst into anger, but on a scale of one to ten—with one being the most angry and ten being the least angry—I am at a 9.9 (I, again, say it with no ego).

Grace has a gentle connotation. I was quite clear I wanted to be just that: 'full of grace' all through my life. 'Space' on an energetic front allows 'grace' to emerge, if we don't allow ourselves to engage in a response to every stimulus we experience. Pema Chödrön—an American Tibetan Buddhist and principal teacher at Gampo Abbey in Nova Scotia, Canada—in her audio series *Getting Unstuck*, explains the concept of 'learning to stay',[10] which is a description of what happens in meditation. When something happens, we get an itch, and we scratch it. Scratching is a way of trying to escape fundamental discomfort: it could be a bad feeling and we itch and itch. Scratching is accompanied with a background static of fidgetiness: we use food, alcohol, drugs and sex. What happens is that these become imbued with an addictive quality. Scratching takes us away from the present moment. It's in our DNA to move away from the present moment. Lifetime after lifetime you've been strengthening the habit of distraction. There is a comfort in leaving the present moment, like engaging in fantasy is one of them. Habituation (speech and action) in whatever you do: you strengthen that habit and get better at it. It could stem from self-pity, controlling anger or low self-esteem. An urge arises and we do it more. We habituate patterns. This habit to be elsewhere is addressed via meditation. She says, what do you do when practising with no habituations? It involves recognizing, refraining, relaxing and resolving. It takes a lot of loving kindness and willingness to stay present. Once you see it, there is no way to be arrogant and it humbles you, softens you up and you get a lot of confidence and have a wisdom guide. Your basic goodness or 'Buddha nature' emerges. 'Learning to stay' is the basis of humility and compassion.

Meditation strengthens this aspect of 'learning to stay' and in it, you allow for grace to happen. When I first got started on the path of Vipassana, thoughts would come to me gathering a lot of strength to shake me. Thought too is a stimulus for the mind to generate a response; a craving or an aversion happens, as each thought produces a response to the sensation it creates. Initially one engages in them and their drama. Slowly when I was deeply entrenched on the path of Vipassana and I learnt how to 'stay', not 'scratch' my thoughts; in that stillness I created the 'space' for 'grace'. I became softer, more 'yin' as we say in macrobiotics: gentle, forgiving, understanding, humble, generous, lightened up. Pema Chödrön says, 'If you want to heal you have the willingness and enough love for yourself, enough trust. Then your wisdom is activated more and more. You yourself say I don't have to die scratching. What we are doing by "learning to stay" is we are being open to our life and our own wisdom begins to come forth.' Which then takes you to the next stage on the journey I went through on becoming who I am, that of 'trusting the process.'

The benefits of what I am trying to explain did not happen to me till after my one-month Vipassana course. Mind you, I am not advocating you do a one-month course, but I think when I started Vipassana twenty-five years ago and kept up year after year with daily practice, I started really living every moment. My capacity to take up work, create, innovate and challenge myself into unknown spaces grew immensely. I no longer operate from my past, but live each moment and take it as my first moment.

Trust the Process

If someone asks me today, 'What's going on? All okay?' my answer always is, 'I am exactly where I am supposed to be'. This answer comes out of the core of my being, because I trust the process of my life and how it's unfolding. I am the plan, there's no God out there who has written my script. You write your own script, and you are re-writing it every day. You can just choose to write it better. Which means you need to have immense 'trust' in the way your life is unfolding. We cannot just say 'this is my path' and then refuse to walk on it with integrity. This aspect gets deeply ingrained when you sit to meditate. This happens because you simply live in the moment and the truth of everything in your life is just that moment. No past, no future: just that moment. The acceptance of this moment is where all the magic starts to happen when you need to bring in 'trust'. You give up controlling everything. We all have fears, but what are we fearful of? Some future event we have no control over, some past event that is now just a memory. What we are fully in control of is the moment: this moment. If there is one quality that made me who I am, it is my 'resilience'. I have deep gratitude for this one quality. It's made me surrender to the moment and also trust the process of my life.

Hägglund says[11] the Greek and Roman stoics argued that all our passions are forms of belief. The beliefs do not have to be consciously held but are forms of practical commitments evident in the passions themselves. If you suffer from envy, you believe in the value of what someone else possesses and are committed to attaining it. If you are seized by anger, you believe in the value of what someone else has damaged and are committed to retribution. If you are overcome by grief, you believe in the value of what you have lost and are re-committed to remembering it. If you are elated by joy, you believe in the value of what you receive and are committed to maintaining it. The passions are forms of acknowledging your dependence on others and on events that exceed your control. If you are hopeful, you believe in the value of what is promised and if you are fearful, you believe in the value of what is threatened. By the same token you are vulnerable, since you cannot control what will happen. Your hopes may be shattered and your fears may come true.

Mind you, this process gets harder and harder when you start achieving more in your life. We start wanting more: the more wealth and success we achieve, the more it expands our needs and desires as well and the more clinging and craving. This is precisely what Vipassana meditation is trying to get you to move away from. No one is really enjoying the journey and once we get to the goal, it's an anticlimax. Now what do we do next? So, living in the moment provides immense value to our lives and also makes us value ourselves. You don't compare yourself with anyone as you truly believe 'this is your unique journey'. It's no longer just a quote on your wall.

When I finally exercised the choice to move away from my marriage and surrendered to the moment, I trusted the process of the unfolding of my life, which I had resisted up until then. I let go of any fears and insecurities I had. This allowed me to then achieve many more things that came on through this process. I became a lot calmer, I was willing to listen to other people, I became resilient, I adapted to change, I had immense gratitude for this process happening to me and finally accepted what my mum always told me: 'timing is everything in life'. I did not cling to stuff or want to control every situation in my life. I learnt to be 'present' to everyone and everything around me. I describe it as squeezing the 'juice' out of every single moment.

Stay Present

If there is one thing that meditation can do for you, it is to 'stay present'. We humans always live in the past or the future; staying present is something we have no clue how to do. Yet, after so many years of Vipassana meditation, all I can say is that the only reality is really the moment you are in. I used to crave my moments of happiness by engaging in fantasy: the fantasy of a perfect partner, imagining a scene with him or how it would be when I would have children, acting out a dream where I was playing mother taking them to school or dancing with my dream partner in the moonlight. These were my everyday thoughts before I signed off at night. As I grew deep into Vipassana, these fantasies dropped away quite naturally as I came to understand the nature of clinging and craving pleasant sensations, after which I used to want them more and more. Now I live every moment to its fullest, squeezing the juice out of it and being present 100 per cent.

As Eckhart Tolle says:

> Your mind is an instrument, a tool. It is there to be used for a specific task, and when the task is completed, you lay it down. As it is, I would say 80 to 90 per cent of most people's thinking is not only repetitive and useless, but because of its dysfunctional and often negative nature, much of it is also harmful. Observe your mind and you will find this to be true. It causes a serious leakage of vital energy. This kind of compulsive thinking is actually an addiction. What characterizes an addiction? Quite simply this: you no longer feel that you have the choice to stop. It seems stronger than you. It also gives you a false sense of pleasure, pleasure that invariably turns into pain.

Eckhart says if you ceased to think, you feel you would cease to be as you derive your sense of self from the content and activity of your mind. Because you believe that you would cease to be if you stopped thinking. So, essentially identifying with your thoughts is an ego attachment, it gives you a sense of yourself, when in reality there is no self. Hard to fathom, but it's true.

I like Eckhart Tolle's exposition of the concept of pain-body attachment. I have referred to this before, but can draw on it again to help explain things better. Most of us find it very difficult to stay present, so while we may intellectualize it, it's difficult to access. Eckhart says we must be able to dissolve the pain body. What is this pain body? It's the accumulation of the pain of our past that continues to live inside you. Its negative energy occupies your body and mind. The pain-body wants to survive, just like every other entity in existence and it can only survive if it gets you to unconsciously identify with it. It gets its food through you. It will feed on any experience that resonates with its own kind of energy, anything that creates further pain in whatever form: anger, destructiveness, hatred, grief, emotional drama, violence and even illness. Once the pain-body has taken you over, you want more pain. You become a victim or a perpetrator. You want to inflict pain, suffer pain or both. There isn't really much difference between the two. But look closely and you will find that your thinking and behaviour are designed to keep the pain going, for yourself and others. If you were truly conscious of it, the pattern would dissolve, for to want pain is insanity and nobody is consciously insane.[12]

Trauma leaves an imprint on our bodies and minds. In his book, Bessel van der Kolk says traumatic experiences do leave traces, whether on a large scale (on our histories and cultures) or, close to home, on our families, with dark secrets being imperceptibly passed down through generations. They also leave traces on our minds and emotions, on our capacity for joy and intimacy and even on our biology and immune system. I remember my mother telling me how, when she was eight years old, they saw their homes burning in Sialkot, Pakistan, and how her father got them all together and fled to Punjab in a rented helicopter. They had to just leave without anything. She was the oldest and remembered every moment of Partition and what they went through; living in constant fear for their lives. Crossing the border over into refugee camps and the conditions they lived in, despite coming from riches, being reduced to nothing for a while till their lives regained some semblance of normalcy. She lived with those traumas all her life and never really forgot what they went through as a family. Long after you bury a traumatic experience, it may be reactivated at the slightest hint of danger, mobilize disturbed brain circuits and secrete massive amounts of stress hormones. Trauma is a whole new field and it has been proved that it actually produces physiological change, including a recalibration of the brain's alarm system, an increase in stress hormone activity and alterations in the system that filters relevant information from the irrelevant. We know that trauma compromises the brain area that communicates the physical, embodied feeling of being alive. These changes explain why traumatized individuals become hypervigilant to threats at the expense of spontaneously engaging in their day-to-day lives.

They also help us understand why traumatized people so often keep repeating the same problems and have such trouble learning from experience even if they know their behaviours are not the result of moral failings or signs of lack of willpower or bad character. They are caused by actual changes in the brain.[13]

This vast increase in our knowledge about the basic processes that underlie trauma have also opened up new possibilities to palliate or even reverse the damage. We can now develop methods and experiences that utilize the brain's own natural neuroplasticity to help survivors feel fully alive in the present and move on with their lives.

The ways in which trauma affects the body are varied and complex, and physical dysfunction boils down to one common denominator: stress. Stress is more than just a mental state: it is an internal condition that challenges homeostasis, which is a state of physical, emotional and mental balance. We experience a physiological stress response when our brain perceives that we don't have adequate resources to survive an obstacle or threat (which is the general state of affairs when it comes to unresolved trauma).[14]

I never knew the pain my divorce left on me and how events that I had gone through had lodged themselves into every fabric of my being till I kept bringing up events when I was in a safe space to do so, like sitting and talking to my brother about stuff. My brother—who has always been an avid reader and lives in a quantum physics bubble himself—once told me, 'Gosh! You must have gone through so much trauma, as you have not let the pain go. Just do it somehow, as it's really lodged deep within you.' We humans are resilient creatures. I'd like to believe it's the most enduring quality I have had in my life, yet the pain of what I went through post marriage keeps re-surfacing despite so many years of Vipassana meditation. You may well ask then what meditation did for me. The truth is it made me bridge the gap between intellectualizing and identify with my pain-body much less than I use to. As S.N. Goenka says, 'Even if you do that lesser and lesser than you did as time goes by, you are walking the path of Vipassana daily.'

The subject of mindfulness has taken over many conversations and is predominant in the emotional trauma recovery landscape. Mindfulness has been shown to have a positive effect on numerous psychiatric, psychosomatic and stress-related symptoms, including depression and chronic pain. It has broad effects on physical health, including improvements in immune response, blood pressure and cortisol levels. It has also been shown to activate the brain regions in emotional regulation and leads to changes in the regions related to body awareness and fear.[15]

I came to a proper understanding of 'staying present' quite early on the path of Vipassana, but actually internalized it about fifteen years into my meditation practice, where it started permeating each moment of my life. If you live your life knowing that this is the absolute truth, it's amazing how you start working, thinking and just being. Everything becomes energy and you operate from that centre. All fantasy, planning, thoughts about the past and future cease to exist: it's just you in the moment. When you start meditating and become an observer of your thoughts, of course you need a technique in place and that's exactly what the Vipassana framework seeks to do: provide you with a technique to quieten the mind and be still, then live in the present. You stop identifying with your pain-body. Only meditation can put us in touch with the transitory nature of our feelings and perceptions. In Vipassana, we focus on our bodily sensations, we are taught to recognize how they change from moment to moment and we do not seek to control them, but instead observe them after which they lose power over us. You learn the art of 'staying present', living in the 'now' and the art of 'bowing to your thoughts'.

Surrender to Your Thoughts

Easier said than done, I totally get it, but absolutely possible. Because you sit still and the Vipassana technique itself is taking you deep down into the subconscious mind. As S.N. Goenka says, 'It's a surgical operation of the mind'. If you cut open a wound that was septic, pus would emerge. Most times we are caught up with negative thought processes. We allow these thoughts to take over our lives, we indulge in them, attach ourselves to them. Negative thought patterns create a pain-body, the pain-body creates attachment to it. We are happy being like a frog in a well: we know it to be our comfort zone (very often). When I was in my marriage for eight and a half years, before I decided to quit, I was comfortable where I was: the idea of change was terrifying.

What we do with our thoughts is important: when you have no ego attachment to your thoughts, they cease to have a hold over you. We have a resistance to being present, so we let our thoughts take over us. You must learn to be the observer. This way you can stop giving them energy: you bow to them and become neutral.

We must surrender to what's going to happen to us in order to help our mind change its constant habit pattern: to engage in more thoughts or to control them. Joe Dispenza says:

> Surrender requires that you give up what you think you know from your limited mind, especially your belief about how this problem in your life should be taken care of. To truly surrender is to let go of the ego's control; trust in an outcome that you haven't thought of yet; and allow this all-knowing, loving intelligence (yours) to take over and provide the best solution for you.[16]

I read many self-help books to overcome my thoughts and become an observer (intellectualized it), but till I actually started sitting in meditation, I could not overcome what the mind would throw at me. There was so much anger, frustration and helplessness towards what I had been through; so thoughts would come like tidal waves and wash over me and I would lose my centre and breath. There were times when, after I first started meditating, I'd lose track of the meditation and be fully involved in just thoughts and lose complete connect with my breath. But slowly, just following the instructions and persevering, it got me to a state of no thought (some but with lesser intensity) and because I surrendered, they lost their hold over me.

In her book, Kate Carne[17] highlights stages in meditation and the thought processes that could take over in them. While Vipassana meditation does not go into stages of thought processes as each person is unique and will have their own ways of processing thoughts, this is still a good framework for those who say they will not be able to 'sit still' or 'face what comes up' when they 'sit still'.

- The first stage is where we are at the moment. When we begin to practice, what we notice is how busy the mind is—how it makes lists and plans, how it chews over the past and how crazy and jumpy and hyperactive it is—like an incorrigible puppy. Don't feel disheartened when you notice this, because you are beginning to be aware of how the mind normally behaves. This is the first step on the path.

- The second stage of practice may arise at some point if you persevere. This occurs when the 'doing' mind slows down. In this stage, it may be that our 'puppy mind' of frantic activity has worn itself out and is falling asleep. When this happens, what takes its place is something called the 'default network'. As the name suggests, this is a series of other places in the brain that become active when the normal 'doing mind' is quiet. When we are in default mode, our thoughts are more like daydreams. Ideas, images and fantasies just seem to bubble up unexpectedly. The default mode indicates the brain has shifted out of its habitual overdrive.

- Awareness: In between the thoughts of the doing mode or the daydreams of the default mode, there are gaps. In the gaps, we drop into the experience of simply being present. In mindfulness, we seek to really notice these gaps and to encourage them.

Pico Iyer, in his TED talk 'The Art of Stillness',[18] says it is important to sit still long enough to find what moves you most, to recall where your truest happiness lies and to remember that sometimes making a living and making a life are in opposite directions. In our on-demand lives, one of the things that's most on-demand is ourselves. As soon as a man gets to a place of stillness, he realizes by going there he has something fresh, creative or joyful to share with his wife or bosses and friends. Otherwise, he's just foisting on them his exhaustion or his distractedness, which is no blessing. So in an age of acceleration, nothing can be more exhilarating than going slow, in an age of distraction, nothing is so luxurious as paying attention and in an age of constant movement, nothing is so urgent as sitting still. If you want to come back home alive full of fresh hope and in love with the world, you might want to try considering going nowhere.

Presence is a state of 'receptive awareness' that enables us to pay attention to what is happening right now. It's more than awareness: it's receptive awareness or being open to whatever is happening without getting carried away with our own opinions or judgements about it, welcoming both good and bad news with curiosity and kindness towards ourselves and others. Caroline Welch qualifies this by saying she did not say 'without judgement', because our minds are judging all the time: that's what they do. The point is that we aren't trying to get rid of judgements, we are just trying to keep in mind that judgements—like thoughts, memories and emotions—are simply mental activities that come and go. Without mindfulness, we very quickly—often without even being aware of it—put our opinions or preconceived notions front and centre, as we have spent our lives assessing, categorizing and judging situations, events, the people around us, as well as ourselves.[19]

You can talk about how to bow to your thoughts, intellectualize them and appear to be on top of them. However, it takes a lot of practice mentally to ride above them and stay in a place of 'equanimity'. By this I mean not come from judgement or previous biases. I have watched a lot of discussions centre around the topic of mindfulness; people discussing strategies. I was also in the same place, seeking a point in my life where I had to know how to master my mind and take control of my thoughts. But till I sat still in meditation and had a technique that worked, nothing changed. The bottom line is, you need to have a tool that's been tried and tested and works. Vipassana meditation is such a tool, to get to a place of 'surrendering' to your thoughts. Only then can you come from a place of love towards everything that surrounds you: people, circumstances and ultimately yourself.

Come from Love

My friend Dilshad always told me there are only two polarities we can come from: love and fear. Most of us come from fear. It took me a long time to get this fact into my bones, such that the fabric of my being resonated with this one principle. Today, many years later, I understand and live this out daily, mainly for myself, but also as an outward action to all those I come in contact with. If you can question each action or thought of yours and ask yourself where am I coming from—love or fear—you will get a simple answer if you are plugged into negativity. Then it's always motivated by fear. It was the fear of not leaving my marriage and what the future would bring that kept me there. Once I took the plunge, I faced the consequences of my decision. That was it.

Research points to how the amygdala in the human brain registers emotion. When we are afraid, the amygdala activates. When we trust, the amygdala becomes calmer. When we are calm in love, this trust centre in the brain is on cruise control, but when we start to deepen connections, we sometimes create reasons to question the trust and the trust centre becomes restless. These questions disrupt the trust (and the amygdala), and the love that once was starts generating fear. Love is also a flow state. It lightens one's burden in life and creates a feeling of freedom where we seem to appreciate things more and feel grateful for what we have. Milan Kundera—in his book *The Unbearable Lightness of Being*—wrote it is a bit like skiing and not 'knowing'. When we start to analyse how we are doing, what we are doing and ask questions, we pull ourselves out of the power of the unconscious into the sludge of the conscious brain.[20]

Being able to hover calmly and objectively over our thoughts, feelings and emotions (mindfulness) and then taking time to respond allows the executive brain to inhibit, organize and modulate the hardwired automatic reactions pre-programmed into the emotional brain. This capacity is crucial for preserving our relationships with our fellow human beings. When the system breaks down, we become like conditioned animals.[21]

Dr Narveen Dosanjh, in a TED talk, speaks about using mindfulness to choose love over fear[22]. What's going on inside of us is directly connected to the world outside of us. This is where mindfulness comes in, defined as bringing your attention to the present moment and recognizing our thoughts, emotions and reactions that are going on in that very moment in a non-judgemental way. When we do this, we can choose love over fear. How does fear develop? Social media, movies, books we read, communities we are a part of, things people say and what happens over a lifetime is all the information that the brain absorbs after which an implicit bias develops: it's a subconscious bias, a bias in judgement, behaviour and actions that are coded deep inside. From an evolutionary standpoint, this was advantageous for humans to survive and distinguish between friends and foes. This implicit bias gets in the way of things. Implicit bias and fear are interconnected, and they affect our actions, the way we think, what we believe and all that we do. Fear just happens, depending on what the mind believes is a stimulus of fear. The amygdala stores all the fear memories. It generates the flight or fight response. Simultaneously, a high road response happens, which involves deeper questions: should you be scared or run (a deeper level processing)? If we practice love, we can override fear using mindfulness. There is another facet to implicit bias called perceived relatedness. It is the mind's ability to look at another person and quickly decide 'how much is this person like me?' We use different yardsticks: gender, race, religion, socio-economic status, profession. The mind decides: is this person like me or not like me? The higher level of perceived relatedness that one has, the more compassion, empathy and kindness they have. These are the building blocks to harmony, peace and trust. We don't ask deeper questions because we are not mindful. How can we be a catalyst for change? It is by being mindful and consciously choosing people who are not like you. It's about being mindful to create deeper connections.

The source of all disturbances of the mind—from sadness and fear to envy and hatred—is here identified as 'the love of those things that can perish'. The key to achieving peace of mind is to remove your love from those things that can perish and instead direct your love towards the eternal, which 'feeds the mind with a joy entirely exempt from sadness'. This joy is not itself a passion, but rather the state of blessedness that provides the 'complete peace of mind'.[23]

The one thing that Vipassana meditation has taught me is to 'come from love' always. One of my boyfriends who had everything on a material level, but was still unhappy, asked me: 'What are your fears?' Honestly, the spontaneous answer was, 'I have no fears.' I know as long as the earth is beneath me and the sky above me—and I have my brain and body intact—I have Vipassana to take me through my life. In every situation, I ask myself where I am coming from: fear or love. This comes from actually having the ability to observe your thoughts, sitting still, not coming from a conditioned mind and knowing deep down inside you that hanging on to any fear is so contrary to what our purpose is on this earth.

Thank before You Think: Gratitude

It sounds very simplistic and too many are attached to having an attitude of gratitude for the wrong reasons. But this is what gratitude makes you do: it makes you completely come into the present moment and be aware and focus on what you have, instead of thinking about what you don't have, can't have or once had. Isn't that amazing? Ashita, a client turned friend—and yes I have many of them—spoke to me one morning and drew my attention to the fact that once when I met both husband and wife, I was giving them a talk on addressing her husband Gurkaran's mental patterns. I actually told them they should even be grateful for the bed they slept on and the food they ate. It's true: gratitude makes you stop in your tracks and not think any more, but it also acts as a glue that holds things together for you and brings you back in the moment.

I am a huge believer of grace, I think I mentioned earlier. If I ever had a daughter I'd have called her Grace. The word gratitude comes from the Latin word *gratia,* which means grace, graciousness or gratefulness. Research reveals that gratitude works as a miraculous tool for helping people who are going through counselling. Mental health professionals have come to realize that having their clients engage in the act of gratitude brings them immense benefit in a short span of time. In a study[24] involving 300 adults—mostly college students who were seeking mental health counselling at a university—who were recruited just when they underwent their first session in counselling—where they reported clinically low levels of mental health—most struggled with depression and anxiety. These students were then randomly recruited into three separate groups. All three groups received counselling services. The first group was instructed to write a letter of gratitude to another person each week for three weeks, whereas the second group was asked to write about their deepest thoughts and feelings about negative experiences. The third group was not given any activity.

What was found was that—compared to other participants who wrote about negative experiences or only received counselling—those who wrote gratitude letters reported significantly better mental health four to twelve weeks after their writing exercise ended, suggesting that gratitude writing can be beneficial not just for healthy, well-adjusted individuals, but also for those struggling with mental health concerns. People who regularly practice gratitude report that they feel more positive, sleep better, express more compassion and kindness and also have stronger immune systems.

A few things happen when we engage in gratitude: it focuses you to think outside yourself, makes you realize how much abundance you really have, moves you away from negative emotions, starts changing mental strength, enhances empathy and reduces aggression, keeps us optimistic and makes us generous with ourselves and what we possess. I always feel we should engage in gratitude without any expectation, simply to be aware of what we have and how lucky we are to have it.

Sometime back, I went through a little bit of a negative spell. Usually my lows last all of ten minutes, but this one lasted a week. This was during the pandemic. We had just had the first lockdown. All through this time, I was still meditating—which means I was also doing my gratitude practice—but as it was I was still not able to look beyond my negative thought patterns. It's when I realized that I should start breaking down my gratitude even for the littlest things I have and make my thanks for even the meal I eat, the bed I sleep in, the clients I have and the staff that supports me. When we think of gratitude, we always think of the larger things, but sometimes focusing on the smaller stuff also makes us appreciate our lives much more. I passed through this time simply by doing this little act of gratitude.

Our lives are actually exactly unfolding the way they were supposed to. Our lives are a privilege. We must be thankful for everything life has to offer us. When I look back at the stuff I went through in my marriage, I always have gratitude for that time. If it wasn't for that time in my life, I would not have encountered Vipassana and if I did not encounter Vipassana, I would not be the person I am today. Even when I left my marriage, I had immense gratitude towards all those who played a part in it (negative as well), as I was done learning the karmas that it stirred within me. I looked at them as instruments that actually shook those karmas up in me and for that I had to thank them.

What Is Your Purpose?

'Every morning, even before I open my eyes, I know I am in my bedroom and my bed. But sometimes I wake up with a feeling of childish amazement: why am I myself? What astonishes me is the fact of finding myself here, and at this moment, deep in this life and not in any other. What stroke of chance has brought this about?'

—Simone de Beauvoir

Initially when I started Vipassana meditation, I was going through a rough time in my life and my attachment to this phase and whatever came up was so strong that I could not walk away with the essence of the practice. As I progressed, I realized that to actually internalize and live Vipassana on a day-to-day basis just sort of happens after you practice daily meditation. I did realize quite early in my life that it was going to pan out quite differently (I again say this with no ego at all). By differently, I mean I would be tied to self-evolution quite strongly in this life. Therefore, after the Mahabharata of my life unfolded and finished—and I got back on my feet with my wits about me—I had also started living my practice. So when I say take your practice into the world, I mean really truly live it. This means every action of yours must come from a centre of giving, kindness, sharing and ultimately love. So there are no barriers. You simply are energy: realize it and know you cannot hang on to anything. Living in the now and staying present becomes so sharp that it just becomes a way of life.

I know if you are reading this and don't quite know how to take meditation forward—because you are in a negative spiral in your life—it may seem like I am talking about these lofty thoughts. So how are you going to achieve this state of 'no fear' and only love?

The first step is also to align your life with your purpose. For me, it started when I took the path of macrobiotics, which became my purpose. I knew it was a calling. I was lucky that when I was in the field of market research—and had already encountered Vipassana—I understood the field of energy and what made the universe work. I needed to align my life's work with this principle of energetics as I knew I was already on the path. When I was sitting in Mona Schwartz's home in Dehradun—and poring over all the research on macrobiotics—I had already put the question of what my life's purpose was, out to the Universe. Sitting there, I knew in my bones that it was to study, live and practice the macrobiotic way. The path of macrobiotics also talks about energy and how 'one universal energy' splits into yin and yang and how food has its own energy; this was in complete alignment with what I was doing with my Vipassana practice. Today I apply my knowledge of the purpose of my life every single day. It's the best thing I do not just for myself, but also for the community, and this is my contribution to the world (I mean that in the most non-selfish way). My purpose has grown out of secular faith. I've already come to the conclusion that my life isn't about all the money I make or will make, but the individual lives I am touching with my work and will continue to touch. I am never plugged into what I have achieved; I am more concerned about the people I meet, whose lives I want to impact and change with what I do. Recently I was a guest on a podcast called *Live Like You Love Yourself* and was asked what my legacy was. My honest, spontaneous answer to this question was that I don't even think of my legacy, as that in itself is being tied to ego. I think I am living my legacy daily by giving back. Happiness also lies in what your purpose is. Once you have a purpose defined as 'a central, self-organizing life aim that organizes and stimulates goals, manages behaviours and provides a sense of meaning'.[25]

The Japanese concept of *ikigai* is well known. It translates roughly to 'the happiness of always being busy', but it goes a step beyond. It also seems to be one way of explaining the extraordinary longevity of the Japanese, especially on the island of Okinawa where there are 24.55 people over the age of 100 for every 1 million inhabitants: far more than the global average. The Okinawa diet is also where the philosophy of macrobiotics is rooted. Those who study why the inhabitants of this island in the south of Japan live longer than people anywhere else in the world, believe that one of the keys—in addition to a healthy diet, a simple life in the outdoors, green tea and the sub-tropical climate—is the ikigai that shapes their lives. See the chart which helps you figure out your ikigai.

Based on a diagram by Mark Winn

According to the Japanese, everyone has an ikigai: what a French philosopher might call a raison d'être. Some people have found their ikigai, while others are still looking, though they carry it within them. Our ikigai is hidden deep inside each of us and finding it requires a patient search. Our ikigai is the reason we get up every morning. So, find yours.[26]

Again, I draw from Hägglund who compares our spiritual freedom to Neurath's boat.

We are like sailors who have to rebuild their ship on the open sea, without ever being able to dismantle it in dry dock. We learn from the famous argument by the philosopher of science, Otto Neurath. Where a beam is taken away a new one must at once be put there, and for this the rest of the ship is used as support. By using the old beams and driftwood, the ship can be shaped entirely anew, but only by gradual reconstruction.

Neurath presented his boat as a model for the acquisition and transformation of scientific knowledge, but his boat analogy can help us grasp the conditions of any form of spiritual freedom. In leading my life, I cannot retreat to an unshakable foundation or view from nowhere. I find myself in Neurath's boat, which is out on the open sea from the beginning on socially shared norms, which I am bound to uphold, challenge or transform through what I do. I can alter or replace parts of the boat, as long as enough of the other parts remain in place, and keep myself afloat. I can even undertake major renovations, but my life depends on maintaining some form of integrity. Even if I try to wreck the boat— or try to refrain from repairing the boat so that it will sink—I have to sustain that decision with integrity for it to be my decision. I have to try to wreck the boat and try to give up my life. All transformations are possible only from the practical standpoint of trying to lead my life, just as all the renovations of the boat are possible only from a practical standpoint that is trying to maintain the integrity of the boat. Even when I question who I am—even when I tear planks from the bottom of the boat—the questioning itself only makes sense because I am committed to having integrity as a person. To grasp anything as part of my life—as something that I do or experience—is not a theoretical observation of myself but a practical activity of spiritual self-maintenance in which I am always engaged.

The activity of spiritual self-maintenance should not be conflated with self-preservation, and it is not necessarily conservative since it is the conclusion of possibility for all forms of self-transformation. For anything I do to be intelligible as *my* action—and for anything that happens to be intelligible as something that *I* experience—I have to grasp it as part of *my* life. Moreover, since my life always runs the risk of falling apart, I must always sustain or renew my life in practice. The form of my self-consciousness is not primarily an explicit reflection regarding who I am, but the implicit activity of spiritual self-maintenance that is built into everything I do and everything I experience.[27]

I always ask myself when faced with a situation and when I am in the moment:

1. Can I just focus on one task for now?
2. Can I change anything about the situation right now? If not, then I can't do anything about it so let me just deep-breathe and let go of it.

Twenty Questions That Could Change Your Life, by Martha Beck via Oprah Winfrey[28]

Finding the answers starts with posing the right questions and Martha Beck has twenty questions to get you started.

1. **What questions should I be asking myself?** At first, I thought asking yourself was redundant. It isn't. Without this question, you wouldn't ask any others, so it gets top billing. It creates an alert, thoughtful mind state, ideal for ferreting out the information you most need in every situation. Ask it frequently.

2. **Is this what I want to be doing?** This very moment is always the only moment in which you can make changes. Knowing which changes are best for you, comes always from assessing what you feel. Ask yourself many times every day if you like what you're doing. If the answer is no, start noticing what you'd prefer. Thus begins the revolution.

3. **Why worry?** These two words, considered sincerely, can radically reconfigure the landscape of your mind. Worry rarely leads to positive action: it's painful, useless fear about hypothetical events, which scuttles happiness rather than ensuring it. Some psychologists say that by focusing on

gratitude, we can shut down the part of the brain that worries. It actually works!

4. **Why do I like cupcakes more than I like people?**

Feel free to switch out the words in brackets: you may like TV more than exercise or bad boys more than nice guys or burglary more than reading. Whatever the particulars, every woman has something she likes more than some things she's supposed to like. But forcing 'virtues'—trying to like people more than cupcakes—drives us to vices that offer false freedom from oppression. Stop trying to like things you don't like and many vices will disappear on their own.

5. **How do I want the world to be different because I live in it?**

Your existence is already a factor in world history. Now, what sort of factor do you want it to be? Maybe you know you're here to create worldwide prosperity, a beautiful family or one really excellent bagel. If your impressions are more vague, keep asking this question. Eventually you'll glimpse clearer outlines of your destiny. Live by design, not by accident.

6. **How do I want to be different because I live in this world?**

In small ways or large, your life will change the world and in small ways or large, the world will change you. What experiences do you want to have during your brief sojourn here? Make a list. Make a vision board. Make a promise. This won't control your future, but shape it.

7. **Are vegans better people?**

Again, it doesn't have to be vegans: the brackets are for you to fill in. Substitute the virtue squad that makes you feel worse about yourself: the one you'll never have the discipline to join, whether it's ultra-marathoners or mothers who never raise their voices. Whatever group you're asking about, the answer to this question is no.

8. **What is my body telling me?**

As I often say, my mind is a two-bit whore. By which I mean that my self-justifying brain, like any self-justifying brain, will happily absorb beliefs based on biases, ego-gratification, magical thinking or just plain error. The body knows better. It's a wise, capable creature. It recoils from what's bad for us and leans into what's good. Let it.

9. **How much junk could a chic chick chuck if a chic chick could chuck junk?**

I believe this question was originally posed by Lao Tzu, who also wrote, 'To become learned, each day add something. To become enlightened, each day drop something.' Face it: You'd be better off without some of your relationships, many of your possessions and most of your thoughts. Chuck your chic-chick junk, chic chick. Enlightenment awaits.

10. **What's so funny?**

Adults tend to put this question to children in a homicidal-sounding snarl, which is probably why as you grew up, your laughter rate dropped from 400 times a day (for toddlers) to the grown-up daily average of fifteen. Regain your youth by laughing at every possible situation. Then please tell us what's funny: about everyday life, about human nature, even about pain and fear. We'll pay you anything.

11. **Where am I wrong?**

This might well be the most powerful question on our list. As Socrates believed, we gain our first measure of intelligence when we first admit our own ignorance. Your ego wants you to avoid noticing where you may have bad information or unworkable ideas. But you'll gain far more capability and respect by asking where you're wrong than you're right.

12. **What potential memories am I bartering and is the profit worth the price?**

I once read a story about a world where people sold memories the way we can sell plasma. The protagonist was an addict who'd pawned many memories for drugs, but had sworn never to sell his memory of falling in love. His addiction won. Afterward he was unaware of his loss, lacking the memory he'd sold. But for the reader, the trade-off was ghastly to contemplate. Every time you choose social acceptance over your heart's desires or financial gain over ethics or your comfort zone over the adventure you were born to experience, you're making a similar deal. Don't.

13. **Am I the only one struggling not to fart during yoga?**

   I felt profoundly liberated when this issue was raised on Saturday Night Live's 'Weekend Update'. Not everyone does yoga, but SNL reminded me that everyone dreads committing some sort of gaffe. Substitute your greatest shame. Fear: crying at work, belching in church, throwing up on the prime minister of Japan. Then know you aren't alone. Everyone worries about such faux pas and many have committed them (well, maybe not the throwing up on PMs). Accepting this is a bold step toward mental health and a just society.

14. **What do I love to practise?**

   Some psychologists believe that no one is born with any particular talent and that all skill is gained through practice. Studies have shown that masters are simply people who've practiced a skill intensely for 10,000 hours or more. That requires loving. Not liking, loving what you do. If you really want to excel, go where you're passionate enough to practice.

15. **Where could I work less and achieve more?**

   To maximize time spent practicing your passions, minimize everything else. These days you can find machines or human helpers to assist with almost anything. Author Timothy Ferriss 'batches' job tasks into his famous 'four-hour work week'. My client Cindy has an e-mail ghost writer. Another client, Angela, hired an assistant in the Philippines who flawlessly tracks her schedule and her investments. Get creative with available resources to find more time in your life and life in your time.

16. **How can I keep myself absolutely safe?**

   Ask this question just to remind yourself of the answer: You can't. Life is inherently uncertain. The way to cope with that reality is not to control and avoid your way into a rigid little demi-life, but to develop courage. Doing what you long to do, despite fear, will accomplish this.

17. **Where should I break the rules?**

   If everyone kept all the rules, we'd still be practising cherished traditions like child marriage, slavery and public hangings. The way humans become humane is by assessing from the heart, rather than the rulebook, where the justice of a situation lies. Sometimes you have to break the rules around you to keep the rules within you.

18. **So say I lived in that fabulous house in Tuscany, with untold wealth, a gorgeous, adoring mate and a full staff of servants ... then what?**

   We can get so obsessed with acquiring fabulous lives that we forget to live. When my clients ask themselves this question, they almost always discover that their 'perfect life' pastimes are already available. Sharing joy with loved ones, spending time in nature, finding inner peace, writing your novel, plotting revenge: you can do all these things now. Begin!

19. **Are my thoughts hurting or healing?**

Your situation may endanger your life and limbs, but only your thoughts can endanger your happiness. Telling yourself a miserable story about your circumstances creates suffering. Telling yourself a more positive and grateful story, studies show, increases happiness. Wherever you are, whatever you're doing, choose thoughts that knit your heart together, rather than tear it apart.

20. **Really truly: Is this what I want to be doing?**

It's been several seconds since you asked this. Ask it again. Not to make yourself petulant or frustrated, just to see if it's possible to choose anything and I mean any little thing, that would make your present experience more delightful. Thus continues the revolution.

Manifesting What You Want from Life

> 'The unknown is the perfect place to create something
> new from. You can't create anything new from the
> known.'

—Dr Joe Dispenza[29]

If indeed we are the sole reason for our unhappiness,
then we are also the sole reason for our happiness. Since
unhappiness is the only real state that throws us off
gear (suffering the way the Buddha meant it), Vipassana
teaches us how to manage this very well. We can actually
be in a permanent state of 'bliss' always. This may seem
unreal to you, but we are or can strive to be the masters
of our own destiny.

I am sure most of you read the book *The Secret*, which
spoke of how thoughts can change your life. If Vipassana
seeks to keep you in an equanimous state all the time—
with no real lows or highs—then you should be able to
manifest positivity all the time. 'Free will resides in our
frontal cortex and we can train ourselves to make more
intelligent choices and to be conscious of the choices we're
making. And I think it takes practice, different kinds of
practice. We can go to the gym and pump up our biceps,
or we can pump up our frontal cortex by doing yoga and
meditation and other practices.'[30]

If everything you are (as explained earlier) is just
subatomic particles and everything in the universe is
also just subatomic particles, then what is outside is
also the same on the inside. Vipassana is like the bridge

that connects the inside with the outside, such that you align with it. By their very nature, these particles—when they exist as pure potential—are in their wave state while they are not being observed. They are potentially everything and nothing until they are observed. They exist everywhere and nowhere until they are observed. Thus, everything in our physical reality exists as pure potential.

If subatomic particles can exist in an infinite number of possible places simultaneously, we are potentially capable of collapsing into existence an infinite number of possible realities. In other words, if you can imagine a future in your life based on any one of your personal desires, that reality already exists as a possibility in the quantum field waiting to be observed by you. If your mind can influence the appearance of an electron, then theoretically it can influence the appearance of any possibility.'[31]

That is, you react to all the sensations you experience on a matter or body level. You could surpass these sensations by becoming an observer to them using Vipassana meditation.

Like clay, the energy of infinite possibilities is shaped by our consciousness: our mind. If all matter is energy, it makes sense that our consciousness that is mind and matter, as the Vipassana framework looks at it, is similar to the quantum model and what it puts forth.

If you remember the book *The Secret*, then you remember the central theme of that book on the Laws of Attraction. Everything in your life, and in the lives of those around you, is affected by the Law of Attraction.

The Law of Attraction says: That which is like unto itself, is drawn. To better understand the Law of Attraction, see yourself as a magnet attracting unto you the essence of that which you are thinking and feeling. And so, if you are feeling fat, you cannot attract thin. If you feel poor, you cannot attract prosperity, and so on. It defies the Law.

Your attention to it includes it in your vibration, and if you hold it in your attention or awareness long enough, the Law of Attraction will bring it to experience, for there is no such thing as 'No'.[32]

After we finish our Vipassana meditation session, we do something called *metta bhav*. Metta signifies loving kindness. I explain more about this in the next section. However, when we close our meditation for the day, we send all the vibrations created within us to everything and everyone around us. Here we can also infuse thoughts for our day, in that, 'create our day'. I have followed and said this every day for the last fifteen-odd years after I watched Dr Joe Dispenza talk in the movie *What the Bleep Do We Know!?*:

> Show me a sign today, that you paid attention to any of these things that I created and bring them in a way that I won't expect. So I'm surprised at my ability to be able to experience these things and make it so that I have no doubt that it's coming from you.[33]

All through our lives we come from our conditioned minds that keep recreating and repeating patterns. When you go through a meditation process over time, the whole idea is to get you to a state of actually not being this conditioned 'you'. Also, when we sit in meditation, it's like you are completely conscious, but actually in a sleep state. Vipassana meditation (over time) has the ability to take you away from any negative states you might experience. This actually happens first. For example, when I sit in meditation daily, no matter what has happened to me in my day-to-day life, I have the ability to switch off completely. This has come with years of practice. There are a lot of disciplines that tell you that you can do this quite easily, but I don't believe this to be true. To get to a place of no mind or coming from memory and past traumas, you need a meditation practice, a practice that teaches you to live in the 'now'.

I am at that point in my life where I have no colourings of the past and no anticipation of the future. I just 'am' and I also just 'be' all the time. So therein, I have the capability of tapping into a potential space that does not yet exist and in this space, I can create my 'day' or even 'manifest' what I want. Vipassana has the ability to help you transcend the body by observing sensations, and then transcend the mind, by not reacting. Thereby, creating this free 'space' you can fill with whatever colours you like: you want abundance, peace, joy, happiness, liberation, love . . . just paint anything and you will see it comes back to you multi-fold. Herein, you can also heal, from anything; it's possible: any disease or ailment. I keep going back to Dr Joe Dispenza because he is the only person I know doing active work in this area:

> The quantum field responds not to what we want; it
> responds to who we are being. Since every potential
> in the universe is a wave of probability that has an
> electromagnetic field and is energetic in nature, it makes
> sense that our thoughts and feelings are no exception.
> The thoughts we think send an electrical signal out into
> that field. The feelings we generate magnetically draw
> events back to us. Together, how we think and how
> we feel produces a state of being, which generates an
> electromagnetic signature that influences every atom
> in our world. This should prompt you to ask, What
> am I broadcasting (consciously or unconsciously) on
> a daily basis?[34]

I followed an author called Marc Allen very
conscientiously as a young adult in my twenties. At
that time, my understanding of energetics was very
limited. The principle Marc Allen was using behind
creating a visionary life for oneself was the same: that
of giving it enough energy and thought to manifest it
in your life.[35]

Marc Allen describes a book he read by an author
called Israel Regardie (*The Art of True Healing*) in which
one sentence caught his eye:

> The Force of Life
> Within every man and woman is a force
> that directs and controls the entire course of life.
> Properly used, it can heal every affliction
> and ailment we may have.

He says we are all born with the tools of magical creation in abundance. There is nothing we need that we don't already have. The tools of magical creation are simply our dreams and our imagination. Dare to dream of the life you want to live *ideally*. Then ask your powerful subconscious mind to show you how to create that life in reality. Basically 'ask and you shall receive'.

After you close a meditation, when you engage in loving kindness or metta bhav, you can infuse the vibrations with words. I love Marc Allen's philosophy. This is what he says:

> *Every day, in every way*
> *I am getting better and better,*
> *In an easy and relaxed manner,*
> *A healthy and positive way,*
> *In its own perfect time,*
> *For the highest good of all.*
> *I am filled with healing energy.*
> *I am healed, I am whole.*
> *I am perfect as I am.*[36]

Living Your Practice

S.N. Goenka, in his discourses, says your meditation is not really doing anything for you, if you do not actually live it. One should live united. There is a quality to your life: if you really practice meditation there is no quarrel. People should be like water and milk together and you look at each other with love, not a trace of negativity.

People should get inspiration seeing you and have more courage seeing you. It's a huge responsibility. Especially in today's scenario, where the entire world has shut down because of the pandemic, we are living scared. Just like a good food plan to up the immunity of your body, we need meditation to up the immunity of our mind.

In macrobiotics, the path I teach and practice with my clients, there is a concept of 'one peaceful world', where Michio Kushi explains how we can use our foods to create peace and harmony. Much the same way how S.N. Goenka explains how we can use meditation to do the same. Because we learn to handle our own negativity, we transcend it and can get into a space of kindness, compassion, giving back and being of service to others. Vipassana meditation will take you to this space eventually. You can now actually start living your practice.

My meditation practice is not just done for myself, but is an act that I indulge in everyday as a spiritual upkeep. Since I weather so many storms on a day-to-day basis, while I go inward on a daily basis, I use all that energy created to reflect outward and permeate everything I do. My own self-consciousness drives me to be a part of everything around me and be all-pervasive. It's only when I practise what I experience and create during my meditation that I can use the energy I have created for the good of others.

I can better explain this from where I stand today, after having gone through a failed marriage, changing careers completely late in life, fighting against all sorts of discrimination: racial (in America), sexual (God knows we women face it all the time) and on the basis of gender. This started happening right from my childhood and continues even today. I would add that being a woman with an intellect and a voice does not help in a country like India either. While my example may seem very small to you, I would like to narrate it to you in any case. It took me time to really get to the place where I stand today. It's been fighting, pretty much since I was a kid, so much so it became second nature to me. There were some tribal rules imposed by my tribe (basically my family, of which my dad was quite the patriarch). I grew up with my own conditionings as, up until then, it was me fighting my space as a firstborn girl child in a Punjabi, male-dominated family, the male being my dad. My traumas and trigger points for anger happened after getting married: needless to say, I still operated from past conditionings. Post my divorce, I was a young woman, a flat owner (aged thirty-two) in a totally male-dominated housing society in Mumbai. So now came the dominating attitude of men who were older, conditioned by their own thoughts. I was a woman who participated in meetings and had a voice, and I was the only woman who attended these meetings; something that did not go down easily with them. Anyway, today while I am writing this book, I am the secretary of the same society, amidst the same men who admonished me and tried to shut me up. The same men have detested the fact that I have been spearheading and doing a great job as a secretary. So the gang of eight-odd members (of the total twenty-three) have tried everything in the book to have me out, including sending legal notices for plants being watered by members or stuff kept in the landing of their floors; meaningless issues in a world that is facing deaths, no oxygen cylinders, people getting unemployed and the world falling apart, let alone India. I have had to use all my Vipassana meditation to handle them. I have tried at every step to be compassionate and kind. As S.N. Goenka says, be a lion and roar with complete consciousness that you are indeed doing so. This is the field where my Vipassana practice is being tested every day. I really try and keep trying. I get punched, boxed down and get up and still smile. I am working hard even today to not let my negativity get the better of me: work with no ego in me and to just serve this community.

I have always lived my life accepting that I could go or exit this universe anytime. So while it sounds pessimistic, the fact that I live with facing the possibility of death, makes me live my life also knowing that I cannot hold on to anything. I may become ill, some work that I am pursuing may not come to fruition and the standards I set for myself may be just mine: self-created, with no one else judging me about them. To lead my highly vibrational Vipassana life, I must accept that I may be nothing or nobody tomorrow. Hence it matters even more that I keep everything together every moment.

Living my practice means I cannot live detached from what's going on around me. It means taking my practice with me to the world, in my life, to my clients. The biggest compliment I get from clients is how I gift them my presence. I never make them feel rushed—or that they are unimportant—and the fact that I attend to them myself. My self-consciousness exists in and through the activities that actually sustain my life, which means

I use the meditation state and what it creates for me for the good of others. It is important for my own spiritual growth—not because I will gain salvation at the end or end up someplace good (not with that attachment)—but because I would like to exit once and for all from a conditioned life.

'Mindfulness is the thin edge of a wedge that, if inserted deeply enough into our minds, will open them to wisdom.'

—Andrew Olendzki

10

VIPASSANA: A PRACTICAL GUIDE FOR DOING A COURSE

The Actual Course

A Vipassana course today is always taught in a ten-day format. If you want to learn Vipassana in its authentic, unmodified tradition you need to be able to take ten days of your life and go for a ten-day residential course. Vipassana also means meditating on reality in an unbroken, continuous way. To learn what Vipassana really offers, you need to give yourself time to meditate all the time during the ten-day course to experience the breakthroughs of the technique itself, because in the ten-day format, you meditate all the time. It is different from meditating with music in an ideal state, surrounding or in a particular posture because meditation in reality has to be unbroken over periods of time as your reality is constantly changing. If your meditation is available only in idealized states, then the time you need for meditation when this ideal state is not there will become difficult to obtain. If you are in a continuous cycle of meditation, at least initially when you are exposed to it, you learn to meditate under many of the conditions that your mind and body present to you through your practice, in which all your physical and mental states appear in front of you, and your initial learnings bring meditation to bear under a wide variety of personal experiences without selecting and claiming only one as a state of meditation.

When I first landed up at a Vipassana course—this was way back in 1995—I went seeking something 'special'. I'd like to break the illusion that you all may also expect when you land up at your first course. If I was to give you one piece of advice, it would be 'expect nothing'. If you go with a blank mind and no expectance of any gain, you will judge everything much less than you ordinarily would. Another thing to be kept in mind is that for ten days, stop following any kind of practices you follow, like: kriya, chanting, prayers, visualization techniques, rituals, etc. Just 'trust' the process that will follow. I get asked a lot if there are any shorter courses for new students. The first course you have to do is ten days long and twelve days from the day you arrive to the day you leave. So, you will have to plan to take these days completely off from work or home.

The Vipassana course is free. Yes, hard to believe, but it works on a system of donations. You make whatever donation you can on the last day of the course. It's like a pay-it-forward plan. Your ten-day stay has been paid by a past student and you will do the same for the next student to come. No one judges you when you make the donation on the last day. Ten-day courses are offered in ninety-four countries all over the world. I have done all my courses in Dhamma Giri, Nashik. This is purely because of convenience of travel. However, you can choose any centre you want. It is advisable to book a course well in advance. This way, there is an 'intention' and you will see that the universe starts supporting you in every way to go for a course. Sounds weird, but it's true. Dhamma supports you.

Be rest assured: you are supported in every way when you enrol for a course. The organizers see to it that everything you need is available to make the course easy on you. Evening discourses happen in English, Hindi and some regional languages, so when you register, you may want to check if the language of your preference is available.

How It Unfolds

Prior to applying for a course:

1. Log on to dhamma.org.
2. Pick a date and location you'd like to do a course at and send in your application form online. Plan this process in advance, as courses fill up fast. You may need to plan two to three months in advance.
3. An acceptance of your application to the course is sent via email.

The day you land up for your course:

1. It's always good to land up early, at around 10.30 a.m. This way you get done faster with everything and

have time to unpack and get familiar with your surroundings.

2. Carry all identification (passport if you are an international student, Aadhaar card, PAN card or driver's license if you are an Indian resident).

3. Register for the course. This is done by showing them the confirmation letter you received via email, with a student number.

4. Collect your laundry tags. This is done after taking a nominal fee from you. Laundry service is offered daily.

5. You will be assigned a room. This could be a shared room with some other fellow meditator. This is a good time to bring up any special needs you may have and communicate them to those registering you, or ask for the teacher-in-charge.

6. Go to your room, settle in. If you have a fellow meditator sharing, then this is the only time you can talk to them. So decide shower timings, etc. You get a time for breakfast and bath between 6.30–8 a.m.

7. Meet people, grab lunch in the dining hall, rest.

8. The course starts after 5 p.m. This is the time you will give up your phone and any other valuable belongings to the course office.

9. Go grab a cup of tea and snacks at 5 p.m. in the dining hall.

10. Meet after this in the dining hall and wait for the course director to address you. The course officially starts after the talk.

Schedule

I have always enjoyed the structure and routine of a Vipassana course. For one, it does not let you think and let the mind wander. So it's great they have timings in place. The chart below explains what your day will look like:

4.00 a.m. to 6.30 a.m.	Meditation
6.30 a.m. to 8.00 a.m.	Bath and breakfast
8.00 a.m. to 9.00 a.m.	Group meditation (Hall)
9.00 a.m. to 11.00 a.m.	Meditation (Hall, cell, room)
11.00 a.m. to 1.00 p.m.	Rest/Break
1.00 p.m. to 2.30 p.m.	Meditation (Hall, cell, room)
2.30 a.m. to 3.30 p.m.	Group meditation (Hall)
3.30 p.m. to 5.00 p.m.	Meditation (Hall, cell, room)
5.00 p.m. to 6.00 p.m.	Tea/Rest
6.00 p.m. to 7.00 p.m.	Group meditation (Hall)
7.00 p.m. to 8.15 p.m.	Discourse
8.15 p.m. to 9.00 p.m.	Group meditation (Hall)

While it may all seem very regimented at the start, it becomes really easy as time goes by. You meditate for approximately ten hours a day. While that seems like a lot, you'd be surprised how fast time can pass. You sign up for what is called 'Noble Silence', which means you will not talk to anyone, unless you need to talk to your teachers or helpers of your course (if you need anything). This also means there will be no reading or writing material while you are on a course. Your teacher is available from 1 p.m. for questions or even after group meditation for quick questions in the meditation hall or after the end of the day, i.e., after 9 p.m. All your servers are students who are volunteering their time to serve on your course; they have been through what you are going through and are there to help at any time.

The Five Precepts

A ten-day course starts with a series of vows. These are taken by you and made to yourself. It's like setting the intention in place to set you forth on a path. You set the tone to meditate with the right attitude.

The first vow is of taking noble silence. Your silence becomes noble when you use speech to only discuss issues with your teacher on meditation-related topics or you need to talk to your servers on the course for something you need or something that is administration-related. It includes gestures, reading, writing, usage of phones, computers; anything that will take you far from the meditation practice.

The second lot of vows may seem strange to you at first and your mind may wonder as to why you are being told to take the five precepts. The reason for undertaking these is to keep you free from negativity. These are:

1. No killing of any living creature
2. No lying (not even a small lie)

3. No stealing
4. No sexual activity
5. No intoxicants

The third lot of vows relate to the teaching, which you will not be able to add or subtract from. You will adhere to it as is. You are basically giving Vipassana meditation a chance to unravel itself. This basically means you will not add anything in terms of chants, visualizations or any other technique while you are in the ten-day course.

Beyond these five precepts there are some additional rules in place:

1. Men and women will have separate walking and eating areas. There will be no interaction over the ten-day course between them. So if your friend or spouse is going with you, please keep this in mind.
2. Smoking is prohibited.
3. No snacks are allowed to be kept in your room.
4. Dressing must be appropriate, preferably long shirts, kurtas, track pants or pyjamas. Nothing short.

The idea behind all these rules is to respect everybody's personal needs, space and encourage discipline. With so many students together, it must become unwieldy to manage so many minds at the same time. The structure of such a course just helps to stay on course and focus on meditation.

You are allowed to:

1. Walk in your free time.
2. Stay in your room during your free time. My back gets tight, so I stretch during tea-time.

Preparation guide:

1. I carry a kettle for my room in case I need to have warm tea (tea bags) or water
2. Mosquito spray or cream
3. Torch
4. Alarm clock
5. Any medicines you are on
6. Bath soap, washing soap, toiletries
7. You are provided with sheets, but can carry your own if you are particular
8. Pillow, if you have a cervical issue. I do, so I carry one that is necessary for my neck
9. A lock for your door with two sets of keys
10. A water bottle
11. A small bag to carry stuff back and forth (bottle, etc.). Usually it's just your keys, which you can put on a safety pin and attach to your shirt/kurta
12. A hat or cap if you tend to walk in the afternoon
13. Your shoes to walk; I also carry socks
14. A shawl if the weather will be cold or umbrella if you know it will rain

I Can't Meditate: Will I Be Comfortable?

The beauty about being at a course is that the centre and helpers make it absolutely comfortable for you. You start by meditating in a meditation hall so yes, it is with many other men or women (usually halls are separate for men and women). For most parts of the day, you are also allowed to meditate in your room. A few days into the Vipassana part of the meditation program, you are

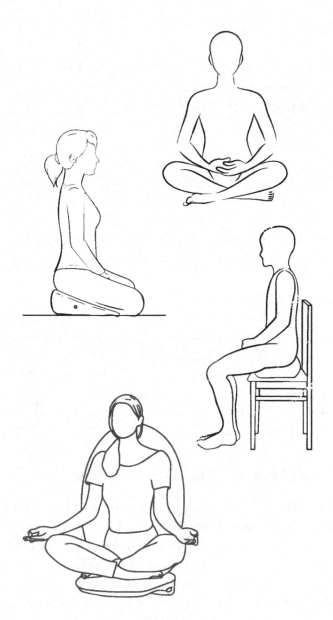

assigned a cell which is a tiny room with a door and a part of the pagoda. You can choose to use it or not. There have been times—especially on my one-month course which happened after being on the path of Vipassana for twenty years—that I felt meditating in the meditation hall alone was helpful for me. However, on all my ten-day courses I have meditated in my cell.

Ideally, sitting on the floor on the cushion provided is the best way to go. However, you can choose a chair with a cushion on the floor and alternate between the two or even a square chowki kind of a stool: square in shape with four legs and eight inches off the floor. You can also choose a backrest, sitting on the floor or even on the square stool (see illustration on page 166).

Reality versus Expectations

The best thing you can do is to have no expectations from a course. Anyone who goes through a course arrives at their own understanding of it. Therefore, asking someone to even share their experience may be asking for too much and it may trigger a bias in you. A friend of mine went for a ten-day course recently. His wife Ekta, who is a good friend, told me, 'I told Rahul to come back a better person or not come back at all'. I just laughed because I know everyone who goes for a ten-day course comes back a better person. So just hold on to this. You would have learnt a tool to handle your life forever in the best way possible. If you make it a way of life, you will survive the most difficult situations with great ease.

S.N. Goenka conducted the course with an audio recording, and all the instructions are in his voice, in English and Hindi. Since the technique was discovered and taught by the Buddha and is in Pali, S. N. Goenka used a lot of Pali dohas. These are verses of the teaching. At first, this may seem strange to some people, but like I said it's nothing religious and you will enjoy them after a while. The recordings use his recitals to set the tone for a meditation session. The meanings are secular and not religious. Most phrases, chants, words and verses used are universal. These are meant to establish a meditative environment.

The vibration of any centre is infused with vibrations of past meditators and teachers—this also helps in keeping you on course. You start feeling this immediately, while there may be some upheavals; mostly you remain calm and keep up with the course.

A ten-day course may not be easy; but for someone like me, who likes discipline, it becomes easy. If you are a creature of routine or can make yourself one during these ten days, it will help you immensely. I like the way S.N. Goenka described it: 'It is a safari into your own psychological Serengeti, ceaselessly interesting and full of unexpected beasts.'[1]

The course is a reorganizing and transformative experience. Most people believe meditation is about getting away from your daily world and having an experience. So I get asked these questions a lot: What experience did I have? Did I see God? Did I leave my body? Did I reach some plane? When most people (who even meditate) ask me this, I feel it's driven by their ego to experience some attachment to a pleasant experience. However, to tell you the truth, meditation is not about an experience at all. Yes, you do go through subtle shifts (you can call these experiences)—these may not be felt at the time—but much later when you are back into your life you will realize you've made breakthroughs. When you come back to your life, you have to 'walk the path' which means keep sitting in meditation to get better and better at it.

A ten-day course is not easy. It demands from you a rigour that perhaps you never had in your life before. This course will take you beyond all the boundaries you have set for yourself and push you to go beyond them. However, it attracts the simplest and not stellar performers in their lives, just those who believe that self-evolution and the betterment of oneself is the only way to really truly live one's life.

The First Part of the Meditation: Anapana

The course starts with three days of you observing your breath *as is*. I do not want to get into detail about anything as then you may make up your mind about what is to unfold before you take the step to join a course. As explained earlier, S.N. Goenka said your breath is non-sectarian and is the ideal instrument to use for meditation at first. Anapana meditation is a tool to deal with fears, anxieties and other pressures; it gives a clear understanding of what happens to your mind when you try to still it. The practice of Anapana is meant to eventually make you have mastery over your mind.

The mind actually controls you on a day-to-day basis. It constantly escapes to the past and future and rarely stays in the present. Plus, the rhythm of our respiration has an intimate natural connection with the negativities of the mind. For example, when we are taken over by a powerful emotion like jealousy, fear, anger or lust, we see a change in the rhythm of our respiration: it will quicken or become rapid. When you give your mind a single task or small activity, it is not used to doing it again and again and again. The mind is used to moving from subject to subject and a different one all the time. Though we feel we control the mind, it's actually the other way around: the mind actually controls us. The goal of the first three days is to give the mind a single order: that of observing the breath in one place, normal, natural breath. While you do reach levels of irritation and boredom, slowly but surely you move towards the mind now being in your control. By the end of the third day, thoughts are accompanied by a sense of calm and quietness.

Vipassana Meditation

'Everything in the mind flows along with sensations on the body.'

—Mulaka Sutta, Anguttara Nikaya

The next seven days is when Vipassana meditation is introduced. Let's say Anapana prepares you for these next seven days. The goal of these days is to purify the mind. While this sounds very lofty and idealistic, you have to prepare to sit with yourself and cross whatever comes your way on a mind and a body (sensations) level. Again, without divulging a whole lot, it's time to surpass everything that comes up about yourself: the things you hold on to, things that govern your mind, stuff that may come up which you have kept buried. While this may sound overwhelming, it's actually not and is a time for your inner self to really shine at the end. I like the way it's been described by the Vipassana Research Institute's lectures:

> It is a growth in becoming a brighter router in the network of peace and loving kindness that we would like to get linked up to in this domain or across all domains. Vipassana is intended to give you a faster and more powerful search engine to relocate harmony and shared joy in your archive pages, without having a lot of negative advertising, or sleazy web pages cluttering your search results.[2]

As explained earlier, everything that happens to us on a mind level is experienced via sensations on the body. Our unconscious mind only experiences sensations, and the conscious mind ascribes a label to these sensations: good and bad, depending on our past traumas, biases and a coloured mind. The ultimate goal of the next seven days to is observe anything that comes up with equanimity. While the concept of equanimity has been brought up a lot in many discussions regarding the mind–body phenomenon, it's in the practice of sitting in meditation that we truly experience this concept; that, to a meditation practice, does not add anything like verbalizations or visualizations, but is a practice where one just observes the mind and matter in interaction with one another, having a kind of dialogue, sometimes unpleasant and sometimes pleasant. Recently I was listening to someone I know, who has a large YouTube following and gives spiritual talks. He said that the one thing he was seeking when he got on his spiritual path was peace of mind and how the Buddha said that one must be equanimous with everything that comes up. I heard him talk and then he called me. He spoke about how lucky he was to have got this interview with an American personality who has a large YouTube following and how his own YouTube numbers were so high, he had surpassed some of his peers who spoke about the same teachings; in short, he was gloating. I thought to myself, here is someone who talked about being equanimous as a concept, but was actually, at that moment, so attached to his sensation of 'feeling good'—craving for this pleasant sensation so much—that being equanimous in reality had gone out of the window. This is why unless it is actually experienced, no matter how hard you try, everything that you read or try to internalize remains a concept.

While you are reading this, I know you are wondering why observe the sensations of the body? You might want to go back again and refer to the illustration on page 71. What happens when you encounter a stimulus, how the mind processes this stimulus and how it finally percolates down to a sensation that we react to with either craving or aversion. You might ask, why do we not meditate on what the mind encompasses? Why go with sensations?

I think my diagram says and explains it well. Our minds are actually deeply connected to the sensations of the body all the time. Body sensations are always there and your unconscious mind is in touch with them all the time.

I can safely—and with 100 per cent confidence—tell you this: that after twenty-five years of meditation, just observing these sensations—be they pleasant or unpleasant—has put me in touch with all the realms of my mind, including the contents of my mind which have been revealing and those that come from my past traumas, conditionings, perhaps even a past life. It is not just trauma that is stored in the body. Wisdom is stored in the body. Calm is stored in the body. Peace is stored in the body. All ideologies are stored in the body. All fears, all ignorance, everything that we call good and bad in ourselves is stored in the body. We are bodies as much as we are minds. All of us can be located, brought to life, met, understood in our bodies, if and when our mind perseveringly, sensitively and continuously travels through the body's sensations.[3]

11

LET'S MEDITATE

Anapana

I would like to take you through the first part of Vipassana meditation. It's called Anapana, which means observation of natural, normal respiration as it comes in and as it goes out. It is the first step in the practice of Vipassana meditation. I will take you through it so you have some practice of it, before you actually decide to go for a ten-day course.

Ten Steps for Anapana Meditation

1. Find a comfortable position to sit in. You may use a cushion to sit on the floor, a chair or a stool. Your back must be upright. You are allowed to use a backrest if you feel you need to.
2. Close your eyes.
3. Bring your attention above the upper lip, below the nostrils and start observing the breath.
4. The incoming and outgoing breath, as is.

5. Try to observe it going in and out of the nostrils.

6. If you find your breath touching anywhere on this area, then observe it.

7. You may get many thoughts and the mind may not be able to focus, but keep bringing it back to this area. The old pattern of the mind is to jump from one thought to the other. Just keep bringing it back to this area. Do not chant or visualize anything.

8. Don't judge it and don't force it as the breath may be short or long, going through each nostril. Our job is to just be aware that there is an incoming and outgoing breath.

9. Observe your breath: slowly you will find your mind will be able to concentrate.

10. Observe the breath for ten minutes and then try and increase it every day by another ten minutes.

Has It Been Worth It for Me Twenty-Five Years Later?

You may be thinking: here is this woman who has written this intense book about meditation, explaining the subconscious, conscious mind, the brain, how enlightenment is achievable by all of us and yet it all starts with observing the breath. The truth is that's exactly what it is. It starts with Anapana meditation. The thing is because it's also become fashionable in a way to delve into the subject of mindfulness, everyone out there makes it about a state or an experience we have to achieve. But in reality, the place we have to get to is within the framework of our own body and it's not a destination or a place that you need to get to. So when we talk of meditation, we talk about how we need a quiet place to do it. We need to be calm, we need to maybe have a beautiful scene around us, etc., etc. However, while a little quiet and calm would definitely help, we do not need a perfect scene or place. Ultimately, it's just that you need to sit and do it. When I wake up in the morning, I don't do anything, I just sit in meditation. Yes, sometimes I do not need to go to the loo, just freshen up and then sit. I have got into the habit of just sitting, with that being the first thing I do.

As I mentioned earlier, observing our sensations (which is the second half of the Vipassana meditation technique, which yes, I have not enumerated here as I'd like you to experience this under the guidance of a senior teacher) is the gateway to everything that has to fundamentally shift within us and make us nicer, kinder and happier people. If you really want to change in a profound way, then this is the roadmap that I am seeking to provide to you via this book.

After living my life on this earth for so many years, most friends who have not gone for a course ask me the same question: Why do you go for a course every year? They look at me incredulously, wondering what is it that drives me to go, so much so that I have gone even for a month. I know what's going on in their minds and where they come from. For starters, they would want to go themselves, but are scared stiff of taking the plunge of being alone for ten days; and two, they think I am part of some cult and it's best to leave me alone; most of them, I am sure, think I am loco (mad).

After being on the path of Vipassana for twenty-five years, what if I told you that it's made me a better person in the following ways (I say this with no attachment to my ego): someone more in touch with just beating to the rhythm of the universe squeezing the juice out of every moment in the day, someone who wants to just do good and is not tied to being negative, someone who wants to just serve people, someone who looks for a peaceful solution in every situation, someone who from being so angry all the time is now the calmest person you'll ever meet, someone who is 'low' or 'down' for a maximum of five seconds at a time, someone who has all the time for everyone she interacts with, someone who looks at another, instead of herself, in a situation. No matter how negative they are towards me, I look at them through the lens of what Vipassana has taught me and reach out to them to have them understand how unhappy they could be and how I can help them change it. Wouldn't you want to have all these traits?

When I lost my father twenty years ago, the grief was 'intense'; there was no start or end of an emotion that engulfed you, but it left you with tears in your eyes and a pain in your heart.

After being on the path of Vipassana for twenty-five years, when I lost my mother this year, I finally understood and internalized the practice. The sadness that takes over is accompanied by complete awareness and an understanding of the cycle of birth and death. But I let the feelings wash over me and observed them—despair, anger, frustration, loss, grief; they finally boiled down to just some sensations my mind was evaluating and ascribing labels to. When I would sit to meditate, I could feel my mother's energy, which I had experienced in this lifetime. My years of Vipassana practice finally make sense.

Plus, if enlightenment is attainable to all us mortal human beings, wouldn't you want it? Wouldn't you want to come out of all the drama we keep recreating, not learning our lessons and multiplying our karma? Of course, for those of you reading this book and thinking otherwise, you may feel I am going a bit over the top. But for those who do understand whatever I enumerated about the flow of consciousness, wouldn't it be wonderful to be free?

While we are going through our lives, there is no harm in also seeking some enlightenment: just a sudden shift in our consciousness in the way we look at ourselves and our lives. So, there may be a series of these moments that finally lead to a big 'aha' moment. I am working towards these many moments and you may now be wondering: are they happening to her? The answer is yes, they are.

My Take

If you've read the book up to this point, then you'll remember that I started the book by outlining Joseph Campbell's 'hero journey': something I have ascribed to all my life. Here is the full text of the way I live my life. I'd like to end the book with this:

> We must be willing to get rid of
> the life we've planned, so as to have
> the life that is waiting for us.

The old skin has to be shed
Before the new one can come.

If we fix on the old, we get stuck.
When we hang onto any form,
We are in danger of putrefaction.

Hell is life drying up.

The Hoarder,
the one in us that wants to keep,
to hold on, must be killed.

If we are hanging onto the form now,
we're not going to have the form next.

You can't make an omelette
without breaking eggs.

Destruction before creation.

Out of perfection, nothing can be made.

Every process involves
breaking something up.

The Earth must be broken
to bring forth life.

If the seed does not die,
there is no plant.

Bread results
from the death of wheat.

Life lives on lives.

Our own life
lives on the acts
of other people.

If you are lifeworthy,
you can take it.

What we are living for
is the experience of life,
both the pain and the pleasure.

The world is a match for us.
We are a match for the world.

Opportunities
to find deeper powers
within ourselves
come when life
seems most challenging.

Negativism
to the pain and the ferocity of life
is negativism to life.

We are not there
Until we can say
'yea' to it all.

To take a righteous attitude
toward anything is to denigrate it.

Awe is what moves us forward.

As you proceed through life,
following your own path,
birds will shit on you.
Don't bother to brush it off.

Getting a comedic view
of your situation
gives you a spiritual distance.
Having a sense of humour saves you.

Eternity
is a dimension
of here and now.

The divine lives within you.

Live from your own centre.

Your real duty
is to go away from the community
to find your bliss.

The society is the enemy
when it imposes its structures
on the individual.

On the dragon there are many scales
Every one of them says 'Thou Shalt'.
Kill the dragon 'Thou Shalt.'
When one has killed that dragon,
one has become The Child.

Breaking out
is following your bliss pattern,
quitting the old place,
starting your journey,
following your bliss.

You throw off yesterday
as the snake sheds its skin.

Follow your bliss
The heroic life is living the individual
adventure.

There is no security
in following the call to adventure.

Nothing is exciting
if you know
what the outcome is going to be.

To refuse the call
means stagnation.

What you don't experience positively,
you will experience negatively.

You enter the forest
At the darkest point,
where there is no path.

Where there is a path,
it is someone else's path.

You are not on your own path.

If you follow someone else's way,
you are not going to realize
your potential.

The goal of the hero trip
down to the jewel point
is to find those levels in the psyche
that open, open, open,
and finally open to the mystery
Of your Self being
Buddha consciousness
or the Christ.

That's the journey.

It is all about finding
That still point in your mind
Where commitment drops away.

It is by going down into the abyss
That we recover the treasures of life.

Where you stumble,
There lies your treasure.

The very cave you are afraid to enter turns out to be
the source of
What you are looking for.
The damned thing in the cave
That which was so dreaded
Has become the centre.

You find the jewel
And it draws you off.

In loving the spiritual,
You cannot despise the earthly.

The purpose of the journey
Is compassion.

When you have come past
the pairs of opposites,
you have reached compassion.

The goal is to bring the jewel
back to the world,
to join the two things together.

The separateness
apparent in the world
is secondary.

Beyond that world of opposites
is an unseen, but experienced,
unity and identity in us all.

Today, the planet is
the only proper 'in group'.

You must return
with the bliss
and integrate it.

The return is seeing
the radiance everywhere.
Sri Ramakrishna said:
'Do not seek illumination
unless you seek it
as a man whose hair is on fire seeks a pond.'

If you want the whole thing,
the gods will give it to you.
But you must be ready for it.

The goal is to live
with god-like composure
on the full rush of energy,
like Dionysus riding the leopard,
without being torn to pieces.

A bit of advice
given to a young Native American
at the time of his initiation:

'As you go the way of life,
you will see a great chasm.
Jump
It is not as wide as you think.'[1]

I'd like to think that I am seeking illumination. Like Ramakrishna says, 'Do not seek illumination unless you seek it as a man whose hair is on fire seeks a pond.' I am that person, living my life with godlike composure, on the full rush of energy.

ACKNOWLEDGEMENTS

I thank my mother, who graced my life with a presence so profound and pure. I hope she played out her sankharas and has found a lighter flow of consciousness.

I thank Shri S.N. Goenka, who is like my second father and who sent me into the school of life, with a bag of Vipassana—the only ammunition I need to handle my life.

I thank Neema Karva, Madhuben Savla and Indu Sethi for helping me all these years to keep persevering along the path of Vipassana.

I thank Preeti Rathi Motwani for the illustrations in this book. I would also like to thank Hanumant Khanna, for providing me with inputs for the cover of this book.

I thank all those who make my life full of pure potential and possibilities every day, and that includes you.

AFTERWORD

The world, as we know, has gone through a 'shift' in the last year. The impact has been felt not only on people's physical health, but more so on their state of mind. The subject of mindfulness has been talked about for a few years now. However, in times like this, we need something larger to help us rise above ourselves and become better human beings, to impact the 'consciousness', not only our own but of the planet at large.

I have practised Vipassana for twenty-five years myself. It has helped me through situations I cannot even begin to list. But more importantly, it has taught me to be kind and given me a skill set to navigate my way through the toughest of personal and business situations. I am convinced after so many years of practice that Vipassana, as a technique used for meditation, helps you understand yourself better and lifts the lives of those around you.

I have known Shonali for thirty-eight years, as a friend and peer. I have seen her pursue Vipassana like she pursued her exercise, diet, career, and as a practice she made it run parallel to her life. She has done more than me on the path, and I have seen her use the practice to face some really tough personal and business challenges in her life. Today, after so many years of walking this path, the technique has permeated every aspect of her life. She resonates with love, compassion, kindness, bringing her meditation practice to help others—not just those who encounter her as clients but also friends, like me, who have had her in their life for so many years, and anyone else she touches with her presence.

Vipassana has been her secret wand, to live her own life and steer people in the right direction. We need to have people in the space of health that guide us and steer us in the right direction—those who practise what they preach and live out mindfulness on a daily basis, impacting people's lives. I cannot think of anyone who fits the role better than Shonali Sabherwal.

Shri S.N. Goenka, the person who gave Vipassana back to India, always said that we should take whatever we can from the practice of Vipassana and let it permeate our life, even if it's in the smallest of ways. This book will do just the that: It will leave an imprint on you, and even if that imprint is small, the author will have achieved what she set out to do with this book.

Sunil Nayak
CEO, Corporate Services
Worldwide, Sodexo

NOTES

Introduction

1. Mahima Maniar, 'Essay on Death Is the Great Leveller', Studytoday.net, 2 May 2018.
2. Alistair Via Begg, 'Lesson in Dying, Part One', truthforlife.org, *The Hand of God*, volume 2 on Truth for Life.
3. Mahima Maniar, 'Essay on Death Is the Great Leveller'.

Chapter 1: Happiness and Me

1. Matthieu Ricard, 'The Habits of Happiness', TED Talks, February 2004.
2. Matthieu Ricard, 'How to Let Altruism Be Your Guide', TED Talks, October 2014.
3. Rajiv Mehrotra, *Purpose of Life*, Speaking Tree, *Times of India*, 4 July 2020.
4. Diane K. Osbon, *Reflections on the Art of Living: A Joseph Campbell Companion* (Joseph Campbell Foundation, 1991), p. 26.

5. Miles Neale, *Gradual Awakening: The Tibetan Buddhist Path of Becoming Fully Human* (Sounds True, 2018) p. 24.

6. Joseph Campbell, Bill Moyers, *The Power of Myth* (HarperCollins, 1991) p. 115.

7. Martin Hägglund, *This Life: Secular Faith and Spiritual Freedom* (Anchor Books, 2020) pp. 4–10.

Chapter 2: You Are Actually Nothing

1. Ian Hetherington, *Realizing Change: Vipassana Meditation in Action* (Vipassana Research Publications, 2003), loc. 309 (Kindle edition).

2. Vocabulary.com.

3. Bodhi Monastery, 'What Does It Mean to Be Enlightened?' Bodhimonastery.org, 4 August 2008.

4. Ian Hetherington, *Realizing Change Vipassana Meditation in Action* (Vipassana Research Publications, 2003), loc. 329 (Kindle edition).

5. *Vipassana: Its Relevance to the Present World*, Vipassana Research Institute, August 1994, pp. 14–15.

6. Ibid., p. 1.

7. Ibid.

8. Deepak Chopra, @deepakchopra on Instagram, 12 June 2020.

9. Matt Haig, *Notes on a Nervous Planet* (Canongate, 2018), p. 78.

10. *The Brain: The Ultimate Guide*, 'The Secrets of Super-Agers', (Harris Publications Inc.) p. 98.

Chapter 3: Consciousness and the Brain

1. *The Brain: The Ultimate Guide*, 'The Secrets of Super-Agers', pp. 50–53.
2. Ibid., p. 54.
3. Andrew Newberg, Eugene D'Aquilli, Vince Rauss, *Why God Won't Go Away: Brain Science and the Biology of Belief* (Ballantine Books, 2001), pp. 22–23.
4. Ibid., pp. 43–44.

Chapter 4: A Quantum View

1. Diane K. Osbon, *Reflections on the Art of Living: A Joseph Campbell Companion* (Joseph Campbell Foundation, 1991), p. 7.
2. William Arntz, Betsy Chasse, Mark Vicente, *What the Bleep Do We Know!?* (Health Communications Inc, 2005) p. 37.
3. Ibid., pp. 77–78.
4. 'What Is Consciousness?' (video), *The Economist*.
5. *What the Bleep Do We Know!?*, p. 82.
6. Dr Joe Dispenza, *Breaking the Habit of Being Yourself* (Hay House Inc, 2010) p 4–8.
7. Alka Marwaha, *The Secret World of Vipassana and Mathematics: Zero to Infinity* (Wisdom Tree, 2016) pp. 64–65.
8. Ibid., pp. 18–19.

Chapter 5: Vipassana and How I Prove It Works

1. 'Subconscious vs Unconscious Mind', Diffen.com.
2. Robert A. Johnson, *Inner Work* (HarperCollins, 1986) pp. 2–6.
3. 'Carl Jung Biography, Theory and Facts', Britannica.com.

Chapter 6: The Cause of Suffering and Karma: Can We Avoid It?

1. William Hart, *The Art of Living* (Vipassana Research Institute, 1988), p. 36.
2. 'Kalapa (Atomism)', Wikipedia.
3. William Hart, *The Art of Living*, pp. 25–26.
4. Bhagavad Gita, Wikipedia.
5. Hari Ravikumar, 'Myth and Reality in "Myth and Reality" – The Bhagavad Gita and Buddhism', Prekshaa.in, 10 September 2016.
6. Janki Santoke, 'What Are Vasanas', YouTube.
7. Swami Chinmayananda, *The Holy Geeta* (Sri Ram Batra, Central Chinmaya Mission Trust), pp. 4–6.

Chapter 7: Who Are You?

1. Maharshi Ramana, *Who Am I?* (digital edition by Sai ePublications, 2014; first published in 1923), location 31 (Kindle edition).
2. Ramesh S. Balsekar, *Peace and Harmony in Daily Living* (Yogi Impressions, 2003), p. 26.

Chapter 8: History of Vipassana

1. Jay Michaelson, 'S.N. Goenka: The Man Who Taught the World to Meditate', Huffington Post, 30 November 2013.

Chapter 9: Living Your Life and Shaping Your World View

1. Timothy Leary via @nitch on Instagram, 7 July 2021.
2. Dr Joe Dispenza, *Breaking the Habit of Being Yourself* (Hay House, Inc, 2010), p. 14.
3. Dr Marc Halpern, 'The Seven Dhatus (Tissues) in Ayurvedic Medicine', Ayurveda College, 7 October 2013.
4. Dr Joe Dispenza, *Breaking the Habit of Being Yourself*, p. 27.
5. Susan David, *Emotional Agility* (Penguin, 2017), loc. 85 (Kindle edition).
6. Henri Cartier-Bresson via @_nitch on Instagram, 27 June 2021.
7. Eckhart Tolle, *The Power of Now* (Yogi Impressions, 2001), p. 66.
8. Ibid.
9. Caroline Myss, *Anatomy of the Spirit: The Seven Stages of Power and Healing* (Three Rivers Press, 1996).
10. Pema Chödrön, *Getting Unstuck* (Sounds True, 2005).
11. Martin Hägglund, *This Life: Secular Faith and Spiritual Freedom* (Anchor Books, 2020) pp. 45–46, 179–181.

12. Eckhart Tolle, *The Power of Now*, pp. 29–31.

13. Bessel van der Kolk, *The Body Keeps the Score*, (Penguin Books, 2014), pp. 2–3.

14. Dr Nicole LePera, *How to Do the Work: Recognize Your Patterns, Heal from Your Past, Create Your Self* (Orion Spring, 2021), p. 76.

15. *The Body Keeps the Score*, p. 211.

16. Dr Joe Dispenza, *Breaking the Habit of Being Yourself* (Hay House, Inc, 2012), p. 251.

17. Kate Carne, *Seven Secrets of Mindfulness* (Ebury Digital, 2016), p. 118.

18. Pico Iyer, 'The Art of Stillness', TEDx Talks, August 2014.

19. Caroline Welch, *The Gift of Presence: A Mindfulness Guide for Women* (Scribe Publications, 2020), p. 164, loc. 1389 (Kindle edition).

20. Srinivasan Pillay, 'Relationships: When Love Turns to Fear', Huffpost.com, 18 March 2010.

21. *The Body Keeps the Score*, p. 62.

22. Dr Narveen Dosanjh, 'Using Mindfulness to Choose Love Over Fear', TEDx Talks, 24 May 2016.

23. *This Life: Secular Faith and Spiritual Freedom*, p. 46.

24. Joel Wong, Joshua Brown, 'How Gratitude Changes You and Your Brain', *Greater Good*, 6 June 2017.

25. *The Gift of Presence*, loc. 1389.

26. Hector Carcia, Francesc Miralles, *Ikigai: The Japanese Secret to a Long and Happy Life* (Penguin Random House, 2016), pp. 2–9.

27. *This Life: Secular Faith and Spiritual Freedom*, pp. 179–181.

28. Martha Beck via Oprah Winfrey, '20 Questions That Could Change Your Life', Oprah.com, 11 May 2015.

29. Dr Dispenza Joe, quote on @drjoedispenza, Instagram, 28 April 2021.

30. *What the Bleep Do We Know!?*, p. 186.

31. *Breaking the Habit of Being Yourself*, p. 15.

32. Jerry and Esther Hicks, *The Law of Attraction: The Basics of the Teachings of Abraham* (Hay House, 2006), pp. 29, 31.

33. *What the Bleep Do We Know* (Captured Light and Lord of the Winds Films, 2004).

34. Dr Joe Dispenza quote via @drjoedispenza, Instagram, 21 April 2021.

35. Marc Allen, *A Visionary Life: Conversations on Personal and Planetary Evolution* (New World Library, 1998), pp. 6, 8, 25.

36. Marc Allen, *The Magical Path* (New World Library, 1998), pp. 6, 8, 25.

Chapter 10: Vipassana: A Practical Guide for Doing a Course

1. *An Ancient Path: Introductory Talk on Vipassana Meditation* (Vipassana Research Institute, Dhamma Giri, Igatpuri, 2010) p. 14.

2. Ibid., p. 9.

3. Ibid., p. 13.

Chapter 11: Let's Meditate

1. *Reflections on the Art of Living: A Joseph Campbell Companion*, pp. 15–26.